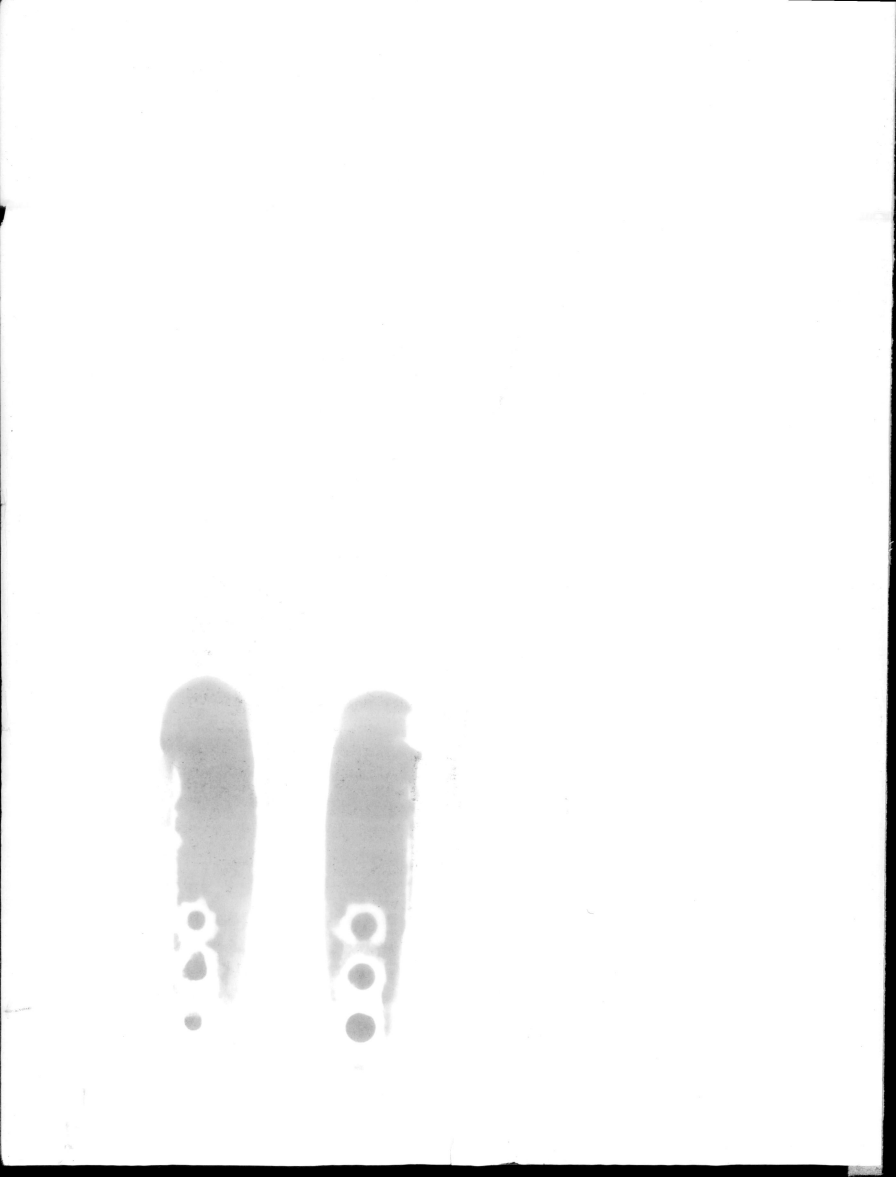

THE
VANISHING TRIBES
OF BURMA

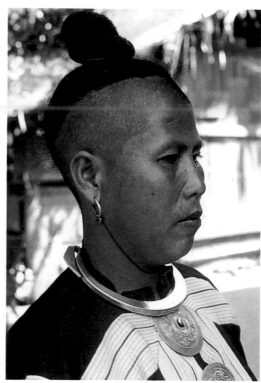

THE VANISHING TRIBES

OF BURMA RICHARD K. DIRAN

AMPHOTO ART

an imprint of Watson-Guptill Publications/New York

Contents

'...There is in this particular region a collection of races diverse
in feature, language and customs such as cannot,
perhaps, be paralleled in any other part of the world.'
Gazetteer of Upper Burma and the Shan States, Sir George Scott, 1899

'We shall never be able to trace all the people
who now inhabit Burma back fully to their original seats,
or say precisely where they had their beginnings.'
The Tribes of Burma, C. C. Lowis, 1919

'Here is a vast country, with a thin population and
poor communications. The races are varied and in places their distribution
is confused. We are frankly on the edge of the unknown.'
Races of Burma, Major C. M. Enriquez, 1923

'The whole country is a mass of small pockets
of mutually hostile peoples, speaking languages which vary
sometimes from village to village within a single tribe
having customs which differ in minor details to a bewildering degree.'
The Hill Peoples of Burma, Stevenson, 1944

'Burma is a living fossil from another era.'
Insight Guides, Burma, APA Productions, 1981

Introduction

By Richard K. Diran

THESE photographs are the culmination of many visits to Burma between 1982 and 1997, during which time I found myself inexorably drawn to the country's ethnic groups. As Burma had just opened its doors to foreigners at the time of my first visit, few people were interested in the lives of the hill or tribal peoples. Although I did not realise it then, I had a unique window of opportunity to capture their way of life and culture. This book is not intended as an ethnographical or political study, rather it is an honest attempt to show through photographs and stories the diversity of the ethnic groups in Burma, and to shed some light on ways of life that are fast disappearing.

Nestling between China and India to the north, Thailand and Laos to the east and Bangladesh to the west, Burma is home to a vast collection of different ethnic groups and clans who for centuries have followed ancient migration routes from India, south-west China, Tibet and Assam. Many of these peoples eventually retreated deep into the mountains and forests around Burma's borderlands, where few roads exist above 3,000 feet, and away from the malaria-infested valleys where their forefathers had lived and died. Indeed, such is the ruggedness of Burma's mountains that two villages of people belonging to the same ethnic group can be so isolated geographically that their language will not be understood by the other after a generation. Chin State alone boasts forty-four different dialects, many of which are mutually unintelligible. Across the centuries, despite a process of constant human movement and interchange, these geographical barriers have served to keep culture, dress and language remarkably separate in Burma.

Even today, Burma remains one of the last unexplored regions on earth. Modern maps provided by the US Defense Department show swathes of land marked 'relief territory incomplete' or 'boundary only approximate'. Vast tracts of the country have no roads at all, particularly in the mountainous border areas. Where they do exist, the roads are made of dirt and disappear into rivers of mud during the rainy season, making travel to the region impossible.

These physical obstacles have meant that there has been very little access to the hill peoples by outsiders. Few of the majority of Burmans, let alone foreigners, have seen these ethnic groups, and very few photographs have

An elderly Blue Hmong couple with a photograph of themselves.

been taken in minority areas in recent years. The Burmese government ended its own studies on ethnic minority peoples in the 1960s after General Ne Win seized power, while books compiled by the Ministry of Culture were not allowed to be reprinted.

In my search to find out more about Burma's ethnic groups, I resorted to historical and ethnographical studies of the country, consulting British journals from the last century as well as studies by military men with an eye to recruitment of the hill peoples in the First and Second World Wars. To my amazement, I found that many of the ethnic sub-groups had changed very little in a hundred years, if at all. Photographs in Sir George Scott's 1900 study, *Gazetteer of Upper Burma and the Shan States*, or *National Geographic* in 1922, for example, show black-and-white photographs of Bre (Kayaw) and Padaung (Kayan) peoples wearing the same style of dress and jewellery as they wore nearly a century later when I photographed them.

Many of these photographs were taken during times of great upheaval within the country. Few foreigners were allowed into Burma in the 1980s and some of the photographs before you were taken while the country was under martial law. I was in Rangoon in March 1988, when the seeds of the anti-government rising

which nearly toppled the military government were sown. Massive pro-democracy demonstrations then broke out across the country, before a new generation of military rulers assumed power through the State Law and Order Restoration Council (SLORC), which was established in September that year.

The SLORC chairman, General Saw Maung, decreed that elections would be held, certain that the army would win. However, the result was that the National League for Democracy led by Aung San Suu Kyi, the daughter of the late independence hero Aung San, won an impressive victory. The government disallowed the results and Daw Aung San Suu Kyi, who had been placed under house arrest in 1989, was not released until six years later in 1995. In 1991 she was awarded the Nobel Peace Prize for her struggle to restore democratic principles to the country in defiance of the military régime.

In unpacified areas, historical struggles continue against various armed ethnic opposition groups. Despite some recent ceasefires, the Burmese government is unwilling to allow outsiders to visit most of these regions, claiming it cannot guarantee their safety. Whether this is due to a genuine concern for travellers' safety or simply irritation at the fact that it has been unable to bring a large proportion of Burma's population under its control is a moot point. Nothing is more troublesome to central government than semi-nomadic villagers or minority groups demanding political autonomy and cultural freedom. In remote areas, many of the hill peoples still live by slash-and-burn methods of growing food and must abandon nutrient-depleted upland fields every five to fifteen years. They may move to nearby fields, or else the whole village may just pack up and travel to new hills.

In the rainy season, dirt roads disappear into rivers of mud, making travel impossible (top). Burma is famous for its vast mineral and gem deposits, especially its rubies (above).

Another problem is the notion that national boundaries do not exist and that the hill peoples are free to wander across mountains as they choose. Ethnic minority groups such as the Naga straddle both Burma and India, while the Karen overlap into Thailand and the Lisu, Akha, Lahu and others find themselves in Burma, Thailand, Laos, China, or even Vietnam. Central government control means nothing to such hill peoples because they have no affiliation of national identity with the government in Rangoon, only kinship within the clan or local ethnic community.

Travelling in Burma, where military rule is pervasive, presents many difficulties. Although all major roads and towns are controlled by the central government, the country can be divided into three different areas. The 'white areas' cover the region known by the British as 'Burma Proper'; they have long been under the control of the government and, under the SLORC, tourists are permitted to travel relatively freely in these areas. Then there are the 'brown areas', such as towns located in insurgent-held areas which have garrisons of soldiers and to which tourists may be granted permission to travel. Finally, there are the 'black areas' controlled by insurgent groups where there is little or no Burmese government presence; here the schools, hospitals and trade have long been controlled by armed ethnic opposition groups which try to run their own administrations.

As a foreigner I used every means possible to reach Burma's most remote hill or tribal peoples. Sometimes I was able to reach them in their villages by negotiating border crossings with the help of local soldiers or ethnic groups which maintained their own armies in the region. On other occasions, I was led to the villages by elephant or by the headman himself.

Some of the ethnic groups were so remote, such as the Lahta in the Loikaw area, that I had to send independent representatives to them in order to gain their trust. Then they were brought to me – often many miles and many days' journey away – to a place where they felt comfortable posing for photographs, far away from the probing eyes of central government. I am indebted to many people who, at great risk to themselves and their families, helped me to gain an insight into these isolated peoples.

Like many readers, perhaps, I was overwhelmed by the most obvious characteristic of the hill peoples – their colourful, exquisitely crafted costumes and jewellery. Each clan or sub-group has a unique range of styles and colours, and great time and imagination are used to make the adornments. They are an expression of status, pride, and art. Until recently they were worn all the time – at work and rest. Now the most ornate costumes are only worn on ceremonial occasions. Western clothing – jeans and T-shirts – are commonly worn by men and children, although women still wear traditional clothes.

In unpacified areas, historical struggles continue against ethnic opposition groups. Despite recent ceasefires, the Burmese government is unwilling to allow outsiders into some regions.

Some tribal children learn to handle guns at a very young age.

Jewellery is usually made of brass or silver, the latter being the common currency among many of the mountain villagers as they do not trust paper money. Animals, land, dowries and crops are all paid for in silver, and spare jewellery on a woman's costume performs much the same function as a bank account.

Although many of the customs of the different ethnic groups have somehow endured throughout the twentieth century, some are beginning to show signs of change. When I first went to Burma in the 1980s, most of the 'tribal' people I encountered wore traditional dress every day at home and in the fields. However, within a mere fifteen years, it has become the exception rather than the rule. I soon realised that this was perhaps the last opportunity to document their cultures. Some of the photographs you see before you are perhaps the last of their kind.

For example, the Taungyo people of Shan State, who seemed plentiful when I first photographed them in 1983, had become very difficult to find in 1996. Some had traded the brass rings they wore on their ankles for cooking pots. Living in villages which were physically isolated, they had stopped weaving and only the very old wore traditional dress.

Similarly, the traditional thick amber earrings worn by Hkahku women are easy to find in Kachin State, but it is nearly impossible to find anyone who can still wear them. The elderly Hkahku women on pages 20–21 were a rare sight indeed. Similarly, few ethnic minority women have had the time to sit and embroider a piece of cloth or weave a fish trap when war is raging and they are left to fend for their communities alone.

There has never been a time in the history of Burma when there have been more threats to the traditional lifestyles of the country's ethnic minority and hill peoples. In the past few decades, countless villagers and communities have been dislocated from their homes due to the fighting. Western influences are also growing stronger by the year and the geographical barriers that once protected them, such as mountains, ravines and rivers, will soon be overcome. Even the most remote ethnic groups will be linked to their neighbours by roads cutting through their terrain and, as demand for their agricultural produce grows, they will become more familiar with outside influences. In addition, the demand for development and economic progress is strong, too, among leaders of ethnic minority groups that have been battling for political rights for their peoples for more than forty years.

As the pressures increase, the lack of cultivable land has led to inter-ethnic rivalries as well as conflict with the local authorities, with the result that many traditional villagers have either left the hills, abandoning their unique way of life, or have been absorbed into neighbouring ethnic groups. The Yinnet and Yinset peoples near Loilem, whom I had photographed in 1987, have had their villages burnt and have fled deeper into the mountains. The Taungyos are probably going to be absorbed by the Pa-Os during the next few years. In Kachin State, smaller groups such as the Hkahku, Azi, Maru, Lashi and, to a lesser extent, the Nung-Rawang, will come to be dominated by the culture of the majority Jinghpaw. In Shan State, the Yinnet and Yinset are quickly disappearing, while the Wa, Palaung, Akha and Lahu are slowly being absorbed by the Shan or by each other. The few Hmong of Burma, like the more numerous Hmong in Laos, have been lured across the Thai border by the scent of easy money and can now be found in the night market of Chiang Mai or the streets of Bangkok, selling their crafts.

The Taungyo wear the same style of clothes as the Pa-O; the Intha are increasing in population, but the resources of Inle Lake will not be able to sustain them for long. Arakan State has been dominated by Burman rule since King Bodawpaya's invasion and the loss of the Mahamuni Buddha image two hundred years ago, while the Thet, Khami and Daignet are faced with absorption by the more populous Rakhine. The Mon, too, are destined to live in the shadow of their conquerors, the Burman, who, over time, have claimed much of their cultural identity as well. Cultural assimilation and exchange can work both ways.

In Kayah (Karenni) State and Karen State, the fifty-year war between the central government and Karen groups have driven more than 100,000 Karen refugees over the border into Thailand. Padaung refugees have been brought into Thailand where they live as exotic curiosities for the entertainment of tourists wishing to see the so-called 'giraffe-necked' women. They earn more from tourism than from their agricultural work.

The indigenous Chin of Chin State and the Naga of the Naga Hills, who have been isolated for fifty years, are still relatively untouched due to their isolation, but even these groups are now being affected by outside influences. The Burmese authorities no longer permit Chin women to tattoo their faces; skulls are rare in the Nagas' bachelor huts as game is dying out, and the tiger claws which once circled warriors' faces are often made of painted wood.

Most of the Wa still live in semi-autonomy in the eastern Shan State and are able to continue growing their opium crop and to carry weapons. But, after decades of insurgency and communist pressure, their culture is now heavily influenced by China and most Wa men now wear the green military fatigues of the Chinese army rather than their traditional robes.

It is difficult to predict how Burma's ethnic minorities – in particular, the diverse hill peoples – will adapt to the complex changes of the twentieth and twenty-first centuries. Determined ethnic nationality movements continue to struggle to find a just place for their peoples on Burma's political map. But in the mountains, what will become of the spirit headmen who can relate the myths and histories of the last forty generations? What will happen to their unrivalled knowledge of traditional

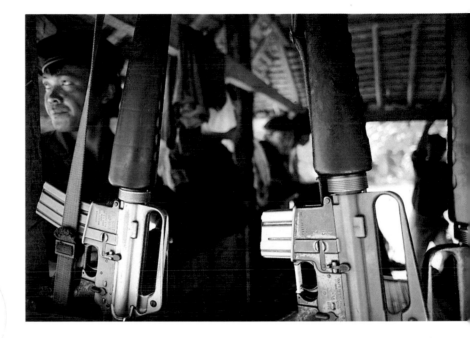

Opium is traded for weapons among some insurgent groups

medicines? Tribal children are hungry to learn, but without citizenship or accepted national identities they remain on the periphery of the dominant cultures in which they live. They have little stake in the future: there are no fresh mountain ranges to inhabit, no virgin fields to till and no untouched streams to fish.

Burma's minority peoples have always had a precarious existence, but the next millennium will bring new and exacting challenges. Some ethnic groups will fight to maintain their traditional way of life; others will adapt and modernise or be absorbed by more dominant groups; others will probably die out, leaving only the faintest trace of what was once a fine culture.

I hope to show, through the eye of my lens, Burma's rich tapestry of ethnic groups. Before you are the faces of men, women and children who are struggling to maintain a way of life that has been rendered obsolete in most of the rest of the world. Their lives are difficult, but they maintain a rare dignity in the face of a rapidly changing world. It is my hope that this book will help to preserve the unique traditions of Burma's ethnic groups for future generations. If not, then at least the photographic record will be there. I dedicate it to the tribal peoples of Burma who, despite generations of isolation, can still offer a stranger a smile.

Geography of Burma

THE varied and rugged geography of Burma has done much to shape the vibrant ethnic diversity that exists in the country today. Across the centuries the great horseshoe of mountains that surround the central Irrawaddy River valley has acted as a defence barrier to the invading armies of foreign powers. Simultaneously, the same mountains and deep river valleys have witnessed the constant migration of different ethnic peoples of almost every kind. Some have passed through, some have intermarried or merged with other cultures and peoples along the way, while others have retreated into remote mountains and forests, where many unique cultures have evolved and still survive.

The different terrains often reflect the histories and economies of the different ethnic peoples. In the far north of Burma, where the Kachins and Nagas live, there are snow-capped peaks which stretch into the foothills of the Himalayas, while in the far south, amongst the Mons, Tavoyans and Salum sea-gypsies of Tenasserim, there are lush rain forests and intense tropical heat. On the fertile plains of the Irrawaddy Delta rice is the major crop, and this fact earned Burma the nickname of the 'rice-bowl of Asia' in British days. In the denuded mountain forests of Shan State opium is the major cash crop, the largest illicit harvest in the world. But rich natural resources still remain, whether in the jade mines of Kachin State, the ruby mines of Shan State, or in the unexploited seas off the Rakhine coast.

Settlement patterns have also had an important impact on the development of social and political cultures. While the Mons and Burmans settled on the sun-baked central plains, practising wet-rice cultivation and establishing great city-kingdoms, the Shans occupied highland valleys across the north-east mountains, where many small fiefdoms and constantly changing confederations emerged. Further up the mountains, minority peoples such as the Kachins, Was and Chins remained mostly in the forests where they practised shifting cultivation in villages that were often autonomous.

In the process of such movements, individual ethnic groups developed a very different array of local cultures. Karen migrants, for example, who passed into south-east Burma down the eastern Salween River valley mostly stayed in the hills, where an extraordinary variety of sub-cultures evolved in the rugged mountains of Kayah State and hill-tracts above Toungoo. By contrast, Karen settlers who moved down the central Irrawaddy and Sittang River valleys into the plains areas of Lower Burma changed over the centuries to wet-rice cultivation, Buddhism and many of the daily practises of their Mon and Burman neighbours.

From this complex past, ethnic places and names have yet to become standardised. Burma (Bamar, Myanmar) has itself been known by different names and pronunciations in the past, as have cities, such as Rangoon (Dagon, Yangon) and Sittwe (Akyab), or different peoples, including the Shan (Tai) or Padaung (Ka-Kaung, Kayan). In 1989, the ruling State Law and Order Restoration Council changed the name of Burma to Myanmar for official international usage. It also introduced new transliterations for many other names, including Bama(r) for Burman or Burmese, Ayeyarwady for Irrawaddy, Pathein for Bassein, and Mawlamyine for Moulmein. Such titles, however, are yet to be widely known.

Martin Smith

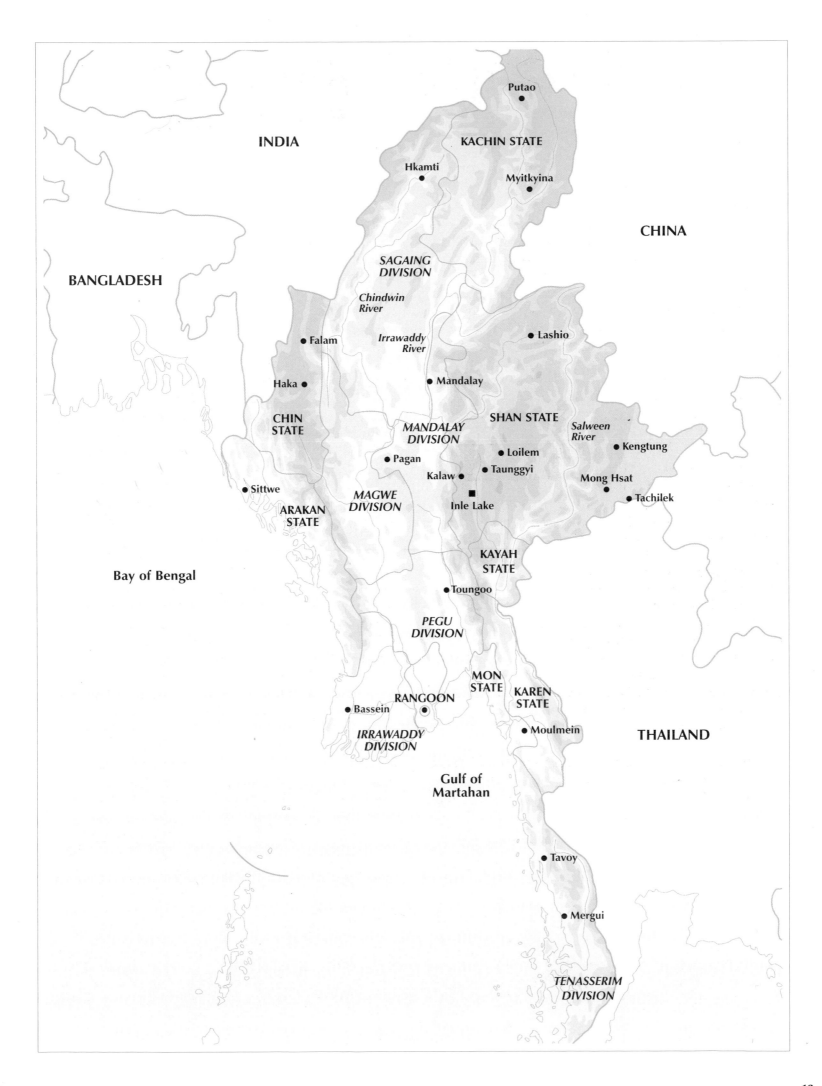

INDIA

CHINA

BANGLADESH

Putao

KACHIN STATE

Hkamti

Myitkyina

SAGAING
DIVISION

Chindwin
River

Irrawaddy
River

Lashio

Falam

Haka

Mandalay

CHIN
STATE

SHAN STATE

Salween
River

MANDALAY
DIVISION

Loilem

Kengtung

Pagan

Sittwe

Kalaw

Taunggyi

Mong Hsat

MAGWE
DIVISION

Inle Lake

Tachilek

ARAKAN
STATE

Bay of Bengal

KAYAH
STATE

Toungoo

PEGU
DIVISION

MON
STATE

KAREN
STATE

RANGOON

Bassein

THAILAND

IRRAWADDY
DIVISION

Moulmein

Gulf of
Martahan

Tavoy

Mergui

TENASSERIM
DIVISION

A young Jinghpaw man in traditional dress holding the hand-beaten silver sword which all Jinghpaw men carry. Many Kachins have never seen foreigners before as the state was virtually closed until 1994, when the armed opposition forces of the Kachin Independence Organisation agreed a ceasefire with the government.

The Jinghpaw

The Jinghpaw are the most numerous of the Kachin, a Tibeto-Burman people who followed the course of the Mali Hka and N'Mai Hka Rivers into Burma. They now inhabit Kachin State and northern Shan State, the vast tract of hill country stretching down through north-east Burma from the headwaters of the great Chindwin and Irrawaddy Rivers. The name Jinghpaw means 'man' in their dialect.

Hospitality is a matter of great pride to the Jinghpaws, as with all Kachins. A Jinghpaw must never refuse a friend or stranger hospitality, no matter what his race or creed. Jinghpaws also have a custom whereby the youngest son succeeds his father in the village, whereas the elder sons are encouraged to set out with a band of followers to found new settlements, near or far. For this and other reasons, including over-population and soil degradation due to shifting cultivation, the Jinghpaw have gradually moved south over the centuries.

Jinghpaw traditional dress is among the
most colourful of all Burma's hill peoples.
Women wear black cropped jackets set
off with colourful beads and elaborate three-
tiered necklaces of plain and patterned
silver discs from which pendulums, engraved
bosses and beaten square plates hang
(above). A woven red kilt is decorated with
panels of embroidered geometric
diamond shapes in yellow, blue and pink.
The hem is decorated with pom-poms,
as is the unusual lampshade-style hat which
echoes the embroidered skirts. Thick,
twisted silver bangles are worn at the wrists
and lacquered cane rings around the waist
(right and overleaf).

These Hkahku women were photographed in the area around Sumprabum, west of the Mali Hka River. They are wearing traditional patlokan amber earrings – an extremely rare sight in Kachin State. After scouring many Hkahku villages for a week in 1997, I managed to find an old woman, Hawg Yun (right), who believed she was about 85 years old. The previous year, I had managed to find only one other elderly woman (opposite) who wore the earrings.

The Hkahku

The name Hkahku means 'up river (people)'. They generally live to the north of the Jinghpaws, to whom they are closely related, in the Mali Hka and N'Mai Hka valley areas. Other speakers of Jinghpaw dialects are the Htingnai and Gauri.

In British days, there were more obvious traditional differences between Hkahkus and Jinghpaws, and they were often regarded as the 'northern Kachins'. They were also reputed to be the tallest of the Kachin peoples.

Unlike local Shan migrants, who mostly settled in the highland plains and valleys, the Hkahku and other Kachin peoples practised shifting cultivation in the forests and mountains.

A Rawang tribesman in traditional dress. His jacket is made of cotton and his hat, made of finely woven rattan and decorated with wild boars' tusks, signifies his status as village headman. The Putao area is home to some of the largest remnant forests in Burma. Tigers, elephants and hornbills are still commonplace.

The Rawang

To the north of the Hkahku, near Putao and the Chinese-Tibetan borders, live the Rawang, another Kachin sub-group of Tibeto-Burman origin. They speak Kachin in the related Nung dialect.

According to Kachin legend, the Nung-Rawangs were the first of six brothers from whom the main Kachin families are descended. Until today, Rawangs still live in some of the most remote valleys and mountains in the whole of Burma, where few outsiders have ever visited. Since the days of the British, reports have surfaced of 'pygmy tribes' in this area, but this no doubt refers to related sub-groups of the Nung-Rawang, who are often small in stature.

A few Tibetan villages still exist on the edges of Nung-Rawang territory, testifying to the Tibeto-Burman origins of many of Burma's different peoples.

Rawang elders. Unlike many hill peoples, the Rawang women's dress of a homespun jacket and turban is eclipsed by the men's highly ornate costume. The man (above, left) is wearing the traditional hunting hat of woven cotton decorated with squirrels' tails. The boars' tusk hat is never worn while hunting as the tusks might snag branches in the jungle. The Rawang man opposite is armed with a crossbow and traditional sword in a red lacquered scabbard.

The Azi

The Kachin ethnic sub-groups of the Azi, Maru and Lashi are believed to have migrated into Burma along the Tibetan and Chinese borders before either the Jinghpaw or Hkahku arrived. Azi chiefs consider themselves to be members of the Lahpai clan, one of the five parent clans – along with the Marip, Lahtaw, N'hKhum and Maran – which link all Kachins. They are closely related to the Marus and Lashis. The Azis live south of the N'Mai-Mali Hka River confluence and many have been assimilated into the general Kachin population.

Some scholars believe that the connection between the Azis and Jinghpaws goes back to the Kachin custom of tracing their descent through *duwas* or hereditary chiefs. Whenever an Azi chief's family became extinct, they would elect a Lahpai *duwa* and claim to be of Lahpai or Jinghpaw descent.

Although they are related to the Jinghpaw, Azi dress is often quite different. Women wear black cropped jackets over a red or blue-black embroidered longyi (a wrap of fabric tied at the waist) and a simple black turban, sometimes decorated with red cotton. Their silver jewellery is much simpler and they often wear silver torques similar to those of the Hmong, and lacquered cane bands around the waist. This family group shows how little traditional dress has changed in three generations.

This young Maru man is wearing a traditional homespun cotton tunic with black cuffs edged in red and yellow and a black turban. He is unsheathing his hunting sword, the scabbard of which is slung on a rattan cord decorated with a tiger jaw, a symbol of his hunting prowess.

The Maru

The Maru are the second major sub-group of the Kachins. One legend has it that they are the descendants of a woman of the Lahpai clan and a Chinese man.

Like the Azis and Lashis, the Marus are supposed to have come to Burma by means of the N'Mai Hka branch of the Irrawaddy River, while the Jinghpaws and Hkahkus came by the Mali Hka route.

While recognising kinship with Jinghpaws, Marus usually marry more freely among Azis and Lashis to whom they are more closely related. Their dress and customs are not always distinguishable from other Kachins, but they have adopted more Burmese words into their everyday language. The Jinghpaws, by contrast, use a purer Kachin vocabulary.

Elderly Maru women in full ceremonial dress.
Their black cropped jackets, turbans and
ornate silver necklaces are reminiscent of
Jinghpaws', to whom they are related.
The jackets feature wide coloured bands of red
and yellow, and the skirts are intricately
embroidered and secured with colourful
sashes, sometimes decorated with cowry shells.
What really sets the Marus apart, though,
are the huge silver plate earrings (left)
decorated with chains secured with a thick
cotton strap which passes through the central
part of the ear.

The Lashi

Like their close Azi relations, the Lashi speak a dialect of Maru and are concentrated along the China–Burma border. Although they have spread elsewhere, settlements can be found in the main Maru area in the lower reaches of the N'Mai Hka valley.

There is little visible difference in costume between Lashis and Jinghpaws, with both groups wearing black turbans and cropped black jackets decorated with silver beaded necklaces. However, Lashi women can sometimes be identified by their huge cylindrical silver earrings decorated with beads and pendants. It is not unusual for the ear to be pierced in three places.

In the mountains, some Lashis remain animists, worshipping spirits of their ancestors and of the forests and rivers. Like other Kachins, many have converted to Christianity within the past century, but traditional costumes are still proudly worn for ceremonial occasions.

The Shan

Along with the Karen, the Shan are the second largest ethnic group in Burma after the Burmans and live mainly in Shan State. Most Shans are valley-dwellers. They were among the first migrants into the area and are thought to have come from Yunnan, south-west China, where related Tai peoples still live.

One division of Shans migrated south to the Menam valley and became known as the Siamese or Thais, while others remained in Burma or moved into Laos. Following the Mongol sack of Pagan in 1287 AD, the Shans established a power base in Upper Burma, with their capital at Ava outside modern Mandalay. For nearly two centuries, they controlled the fertile rice land around the middle reaches of the Irrawaddy and expanded into Kachin State and along the Chindwin River.

Their traditional *sawbwas* or princes were recognised by the British in the nineteenth century in the process of annexation, but in 1959 they signed an agreement with General Ne Win's government renouncing all their hereditary rights. Fighting, however, between the central government and various Shan resistance movements has continued sporadically until today.

Shan children from Shan State in northern Burma. The girl above is wearing *thanaka* paste, made from the soft outer bark of the *thanaka* tree which is ground and mixed with water. Women and children smear the paste over their faces and arms to provide a combined sunscreen and skin conditioner. Temperatures in Shan State can fall sharply, especially at night, hence the woollen scarf worn under the hat (opposite).

The Yao

The Yao, a Sino-Tibetan people, can be found in Yunnan, Laos, Vietnam, northern Thailand and a few remote areas in Burma's borderlands. Generally, they call themselves Mien but they are also known as Man in Vietnam and Laos.

Many Yaos speak Chinese and, as a result, are one of the most prosperous hill peoples in the region. They have a custom of adopting children from poorer tribes, such as the Akhas, Lisus or Lahus, who are raised as Yaos. They never allow their own children to be adopted by other ethnic groups.

The Yao are great deer-hunters, hunting with crossbows and home-made rifles. They are also skilled metal workers, making intricate silver ornaments to wear and barrels of rifles which they sell to villagers of other tribes.

Yao women high in the mountains of Shan State wear
blue-black turbans, which are sometimes decorated
with geometric embroidered designs (left) and a black
tunic split at the waist which has a deep red collar.

Women spend much of their time weaving and Yao cloth is highly prized because of its intricately embroidered designs (above). It is used for everyday clothes, including longyis, trousers, sashes, shoulder bags and babies' slings (opposite, left and top right). On special occasions, women wear rectangular silver medallions (left), to emphasise their wealth and standing in the village. On such occasions, they will offer guests traditional biscuits made of grains, cut into leaf shapes (opposite, below).

A Blue Hmong man wearing traditional dress of a black silk jacket embroidered with geometric flower shapes, and a black skull cap adorned with a red crest. Unlike many tribesmen, Hmong men wear a great deal of jewellery, such as this four-banded silver torque and beaded necklace threaded with silver coins. The designations 'Blue' and 'White' refer to the differences in the colour of their clothing.

The Hmong

The Hmong (or Meo) came from in south China and possibly before that from the mountains of Central Asia. They are said to be the remnants of a very ancient people who, like the related Yaos, occupied central China before the Chinese arrived. Possessing a patrilineal clan system, they fanned out over centuries into Yunnan, Laos, Vietnam, Thailand and Burma's borderlands. Hmong legend tells of their original home being an icy land and even today they embroider a snowflake motif on their tunics and skirts, although the Hmong in Burma have not seen snow for centuries.

The Hmong live on the highest mountains in eastern Shan State and near the Thai border, cultivating chilli, corn and opium. The richest opium farmers take more than one wife if they can afford the bride price and own enough to support the family.

Hmong women are famous throughout South-east Asia for their exquisite embroidery.

A Blue Hmong girl wearing a traditional silver torque (opposite), a sign of her family's considerable wealth. Teenage girls from eastern Shan State near the Thai border (above) dressed in their finest costumes; their jackets are made of indigo blue-black cotton or silk with embroidered sleeves and appliquéd lapels in distinctive geometric designs. The jackets are worn over a matching embroidered skirt and leggings.

Blue Hmong girls walking into the forest in Shan State. Note the incredible detail of their costumes; even the backs of their jackets and hems of their leggings are embroidered (opposite). Their hairstyles (right) are also highly distinctive: the hair is swept to the crown in an enormous bun and covered in fine black gauze. It is secured with colourful beads and sometimes pink sashes. Earrings are made of delicate silverwork (below).

White Hmong girls in a typical house in the border village of
Ban Hin Taek, former stronghold of opium warlord, Khun Sa
(above). The girls opposite are practising a ceremonial dance
for New Year, in which they stand in a row opposite the boys
and toss a ball to one another. Unlike the Blue Hmong, the
White Hmong wear head-dresses decorated with silver coins
and red pom-poms reminiscent of the Jinghpaws in Kachin
State. The elaborate sashes are also decorated with silver coins
(overleaf) and they wear silver pendants, torques and aprons
decorated with colourful plastic bells.

A White Hmong girl of marriageable age (left) dressed in her ceremonial best. Festivals such as the New Year are important times for young girls, as it is one of the few opportunities they have to meet eligible men and show off their jewellery (below), and intricately embroidered clothes (opposite) which are testimony to their practical and artistic skills.

Opium and Smoking

Many of Burma's hill peoples cultivate opium as a cash-crop, mostly in the Shan State. About half the refined heroin on America's streets comes from the Golden Triangle region of Laos, Burma and Thailand. Burma is the biggest exporter of illicit raw opium, producing over 2,000 tons each year.

As well as providing the only real income for villagers in war-zones, the opium trade has long provided funds for insurgent armies in the hills. Much of the opium region is controlled by armed opposition groups, some of which have agreed ceasefires with the government. Independent war-lords also survive, the most notorious being Chan Shi-Fu – better known as Khun Sa – who controlled a 'Mong Tai Army' of 15,000 soldiers until he made a private deal with the government in 1996.

Opium is the major cash crop of the Blue Hmong in the Golden Triangle of south-eastern Shan State, and the women work in opium fields at an altitude of 4,000 ft (above). The bulb of the opium poppy (*papaver somniferum*) is scored with a three-pronged sickle to bleed the white opium juice (left); by the next day, the juice has turned into amber and is ready to be scraped off the bulb. Once harvested, it is wrapped in banana leaves and sold or smoked by the villagers, often as a pain-killer or for medicinal purposes.

Overleaf: elderly Chin women in southern Chin State enjoy smoking tobacco together. The teardrop patterns of the facial tattoos on the woman on the left show that she is Chin Bok, while the denser dot-and-dash markings of the woman on the right indicate that she is a Chin Bon.

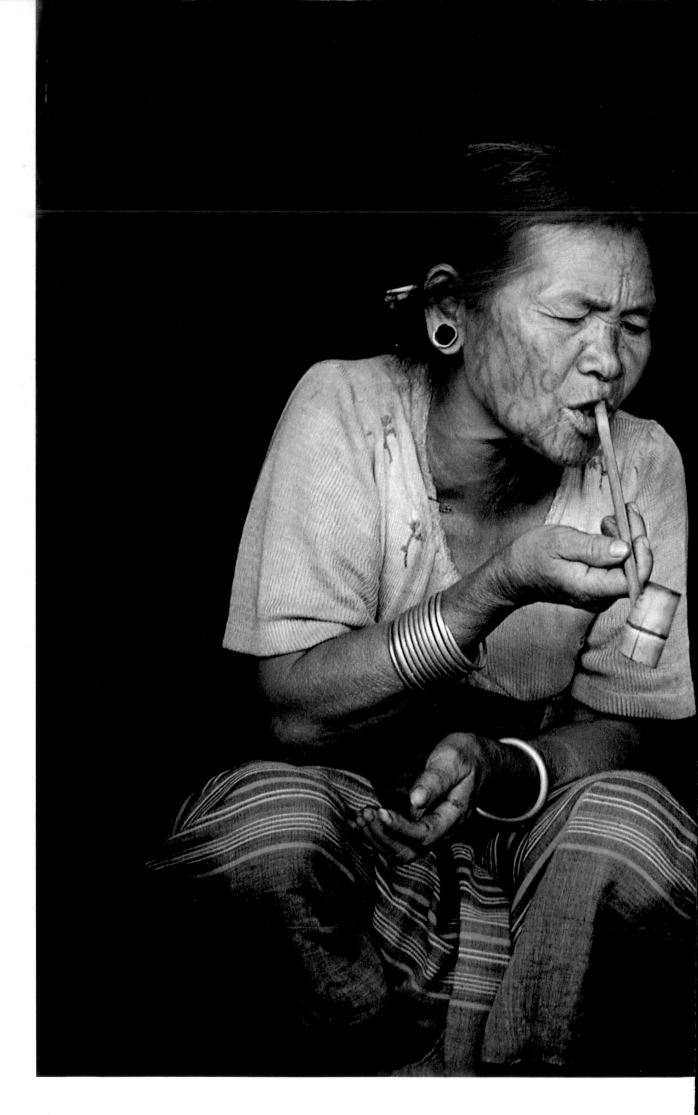

A man smoking marijuana in a *bong*, the traditional bamboo pipe (left). Water in the lower part of the pipe cools the smoke as it is drawn through the wide section of bamboo which covers the mouth and lower part of the face. Opium weights and a scale for weighing the drug (below): the weights are cast in bronze and commonly depict either the Burmese *hintha* (mythical bird) or *chinthe* (mythical lion). Some of the rarer weights feature tigers, snails and monkeys.

The days of elegant opium-smoking, when dissolute young men reclined in opium parlours smoking ivory, jade, ebony or tortoiseshell pipes, are long gone. Here an opium addict heats the drug over a crude flame and draws it through a length of bamboo (above). An old Kuomintang Chinese soldier (left) smokes tobacco; he was probably driven into Burma when Chiang Kai-shek's Nationalist armies were defeated by Chairman Mao's Communist armies in 1949.

The feet of a Panthay woman from Taunggyi in Shan State. She said she was over 90 years old and had had her feet bound in 1904, just seven years before the end of the Manchu dynasty, when the practice was outlawed. From an early age, the toes are trained back on themselves, leaving only the big toe pointing forward, giving the impression of tiny, child-like feet. The feet are then wrapped in swathes of white and blue cloth, fitted into red conical slippers, and covered with black silk shoes.

The Panthay

The Panthays – or Hui-Hui – are Chinese Muslims who originally came to Burma as muleteers on the trade routes between China and Burma. They are thought to have mixed origins, most likely as descendants of Persian, Arab and Central-Asian Muslim traders who migrated to China in the thirteenth and fourteenth centuries and became naturalised. The Panthays became famous as caravan drivers, taking goods from China as far south as Rangoon and Moulmein. Their main occupation was trade, and they often used slaves to carry out their domestic work.

Along with other Chinese descendants, Burma's Panthays can be found in scattered settlements in the Shan State, including the Wa and Kokang sub-states near the Chinese border.

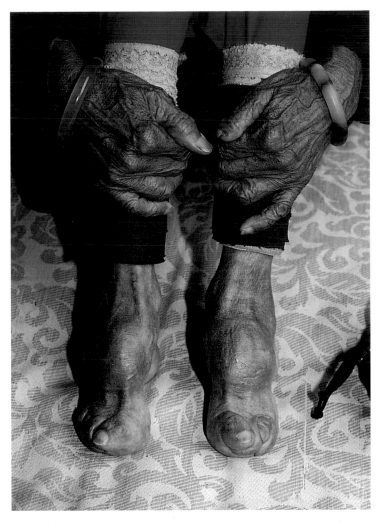

A young Lisu girl from Laukhaung, north-east of Myitkyina, wearing her New Year costume. The most distinctive feature of the Lisu traditional dress is the elaborate head-dress decorated with silver baubles, chains, and long multi-coloured threads of cotton with red pom-pom tails. The silver necklace reflects the design of the head-dress. The simple black Lisu jacket is decorated with broad red and yellow panels and is worn over a colourful tunic secured with a sash.

The Lisu

A Tibeto-Burman people, the Lisu believe that they are the only humans to have survived the great flood, and claim eastern Tibet as their original homeland. They are spread across mountains in the area, in western Yunnan and in scattered communities in both the Kachin and Shan States down to the Thai border, where many have continued to cross. It is not uncommon for Lisu men to speak several languages, including Chinese.

These Lisus were photographed in a village in Kachin State, high in the mountains, up through the clouds where the temperatures are cool. Lisus always choose inaccessible spots for their villages on ridges or mountain tops, hidden among thickets of fir and bamboos, which can be easily defended.

They were celebrating the New Year, when village girls wear their finest costumes and jewellery to catch the eye of potential husbands, and a huge feast is held for the whole village, with drinking and dancing lasting several days.

This elaborate jewellery forms part of the dress of Lisus in the Chinese borderland area. The round bosses of the necklace's central panel (above) are engraved with a star sign and resemble ancient Celtic brooches. The Indian rupees, some of which date back to 1885, are a clue to ancient trading links between the Lisus and Indian merchants. Their skill and craftsmanship can be seen in the fish and butterfly motifs in the elaborate pendant (opposite).

Young and old Lisu women in everyday dress. Bright, primary colours are favoured by Lisu clans, with embroidered and appliquéd stripes (opposite, below). Lisus in Bhamo wear black or blue-black turbans (opposite, above), strings of beads, cowrie shells and hooped silver earrings.

Lisu girls and boys performing the
traditional New Year's dance (opposite).
Dancing begins at sunset at one house
and progresses to every house in
the village. Girls and boys start off the
dancing, circling musicians playing a *ken*
(gourd-flute) and a guitar. The guitar
is made from a small, round drum over
which a python skin and three wire
strings are stretched. When the dancing
stops, girls offer the boys and men glasses
of local whisky. Lisu girls frequently
marry young, as this young mother and
child testify.

Shwe Palaung women near Kengtung in eastern Shan State. They are wearing traditional cropped jackets, decorated with strings of beads, over striped longyis and lacquered cane bands. The jewellery is elaborate and includes silver coins sewn on to jacket sleeves, wide silver waist-bands and silver torques, bangles and pendant earrings. The head-dress of the woman on the left in the group signifies that she is married. Pale Palaung dress (below, right) has slight variations, including embroidered sleeves, red lapels decorated with sequins and embossed silver plaques.

The Palaung

The Palaung – or Ta-ang as they call themselves – are descended from Mon-Khmer stock. They live mainly in the mountains of northern Shan State, where they are famous for cultivating tea. The Burmans and Shans divide them into Shwe (Gold) and Pale (Silver) Palaungs on the basis of their dress.

Although retaining many aspects of traditional spirit worship, most Palaungs practise Buddhism and there are monasteries in almost every village. Many communities, however, have been badly affected by the armed conflict of the past thirty years.

These Palaungs live in Pin Ne Bang village above Kalaw in western Shan State and can be seen regularly in Kalaw market. Their costume is one of the most colourful of all the hill-tribes. Women wear red, pink, black and blue jackets over a red striped longyi. Like Kachin women, Palaungs also wear lacquered bamboo hoops around the waist when they are married, as well as silver torques and heavy strings of beads.

Pale Palaung women from Kalaw showing off
their magnificent head-dresses. For married women,
these consist of woven lengths of cotton wound
around a beaded skull cap (opposite, left), while
unmarried women wear a black hat embroidered
with a star shape surrounded by multicoloured
pom-poms (above, left). Their skirts derive the red
colour from a dye made from the pounded roots
of a local tree. Palaung villages (above) consist of
thatched wooden houses built on stilts with
hitching posts outside for mules. The Palaungs are
famous as tea cultivators and mules are the
easiest way to negotiate the mountainous terrain of
the tea plantations.

The Pa-O

The Pa-O – or Taungthu as they are known by Burmans – are the second most numerous ethnic group in the Shan State after the Shans themselves. They are an important branch of the Karen ethnic family and speak a related language, although many Pa-Os in the Shan State are unaware of any connection. Local legend claims that they fled north to Shan State from the Mon city of Thaton, in Lower Burma, after the overthrow of the Mon King Manuha in the eleventh century by King Anawrahta of Pagan. Itinerant traders and Buddhists, many today live in the mountains around Taunggyi and Kalaw in western Shan State, where their main cash crop is the *thanapet* leaf from cordia trees, used for rolling Burma's traditional cigar, the cheroot.

Pa-O men wear loose-fitting trousers, jackets and turbans like the Shans, but they always dress in black. The women wear longyis, long sleeveless shirts and cropped long-sleeved jackets, but with a brightly coloured turban.

Pa-O women and men at Non Dai
market outside Kalaw. Both wear
the same dress, a black and blue
tunic and a brightly coloured turban.
The turbans are often no more
than scarves or towels bought at
local markets (opposite and above),
which are then tied into an
individual style by the wearer.

A young Taungyo woman in traditional dress, a rare sight as many younger people have abandoned their ethnic costume for Western clothes. Like many peoples in Shan State, Taungyo men and women like to cap their teeth in gold, which is often regarded as a mark of beauty and wealth.

The Taungyo

The little-known Taungyo are an enigma in Shan State. Like the local Inthas and Danus, they appear to speak a dialect of Burmese, but they are also influenced by the culture and speech of the Shans and Pa-Os among whom they live. A number live in the hills in the Heho region above Inle Lake. According to Sir J. G. Scott they may have been refugees from Tavoy in Mon State, south-east Burma, or have been brought as slaves to Shan State, where they soon intermarried with locals.

These photographs were taken in the Taungyo village of Ton Pak outside Kalaw, which the Burmese police had warned us not to visit because it was said to be unsafe.

Taungyo men wear a costume similar to the Shans, but the women are easily distinguishable by their heavy silver earrings and bracelets. They also wear heavy brass coils on their legs. If they are married, the rings are worn just under the knee; if they are single, they wear silver rings around the ankles.

Taungyo women at work and leisure. The elderly women above are winnowing rice on woven platters and wearing everyday black tunics and blue turbans. The brass rings worn beneath the knee signify that they are married. The woman on the left is wearing traditional Taungyo drum-shaped earrings. Elderly women care for the village children while the younger women work in the fields (opposite). Note that the child is wearing Western clothes, which is increasingly common among all ethnic groups.

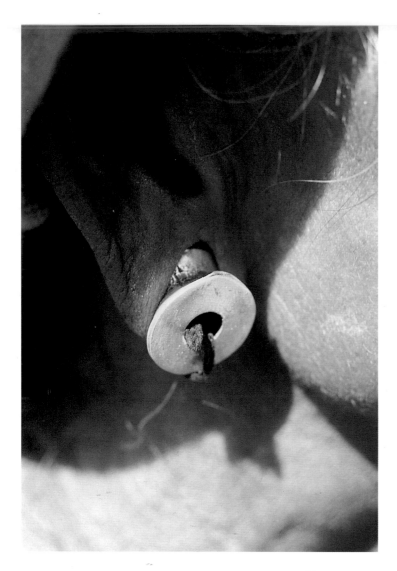

Jewellery is an important distinguishing feature among tribes.
Taungyos can be recognised by their traditional drum-shaped silver
earrings (above, left), which were once a common sight among
tribeswomen. As well as the distinctive brass leg rings (opposite, below),
Taungyo women also wear rather stylish heavy silver bangles
which have a scroll design at each end (opposite, top).

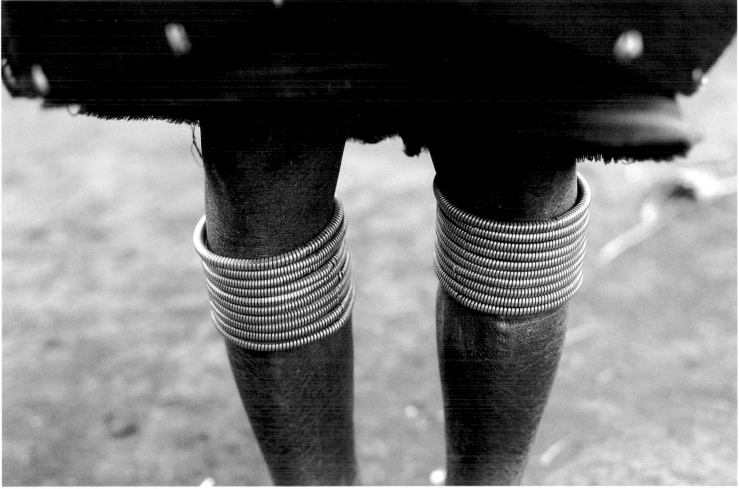

This Yinnet (Black Riang) girl is wearing traditional conical silver earrings strung with beads and coloured pom-poms. Her dark blue velvet smock is decorated with sequins and tassles of multi-coloured cotton thread.

The Riang

Very little has been recorded of the early history of the Riang, who live scattered in small areas of Shan State. They are thought to be related to the Was and Palaungs, although many also speak Shan. Some scholars believe they are southern relations of the Palaungs; while others say they are Karens.

The Riang are divided into three main clans, including the Yinnet or Black Riang and the Yinset or Striped Riang. It is the custom for men and women of both clans to have their four front teeth capped in gold which is then inlaid with ruby and green jade. This is regarded as a mark of great beauty. Yinnet girls wear lacquered hoops around their waists and silver discs strung with colourful beads in their ears, while Yinset boys wear tufts of cotton on their shirts.

Yinset (Striped Riang) boys from Loilem in Shan State. Both unmarried boys and girls wear huge and colourful pom-poms in their ears to show they are of marriageable age. Yinset dress is less elaborate than Yinnet, although men are sometimes very creative with their head-dresses, as this photograph shows.

Yinset women wear a black smock decorated with pink embroidered bands and
a central panel threaded with tiny cowry shells and long strands of multi-coloured
cotton. The large head-dress is black with red and white stripes and sometimes
unmarried girls wear flowers behind their ears. Yinset boys and girls both have their
four front teeth capped with gold and inset with jade and ruby – a sign of wealth
and beauty.

A woman wearing the Akha head-dress; the baubles are made either by beating two silver coins into semi-spherical shapes and welding them together, or by pouring molten silver into a mould made from buffalo horn. Note the red toothbrush: this woman had no idea what it was used for and simply found its colour and shape attractive. Akhas villages (overleaf) are protected by 'spirit gates', thought to separate the human world from spirit realms.

The Akha

The Akha (or Kaw) originated in Yunnan, in southern China, and live in south-east Shan State, on the borderlands of China, Laos and Thailand. They are said to be divided into seven clans, representing seven brothers from whom all Akhas reputedly derive. Descendants of the ancient Lolo peoples, they speak a Tibeto-Burman language, related to both Lahu and Lisu.

Many Akhas are found near Kengtung, where they live high in the mountains, cultivating maize, tobacco, sugar cane and opium. They can also be found in northern Thailand, Laos and Yunnan. Their villages are frequently among the poorest in the region.

The Akha are famous for their women's striking head-dresses, which differ from clan to clan and resemble heavy silver helmets. They consist of rows of heavy silver baubles interspersed with beads which are sewn on to a bamboo cap. They also wear embroidered blue and black leggings to protect themselves from leeches, which fall off the wet leaves and puncture the skin.

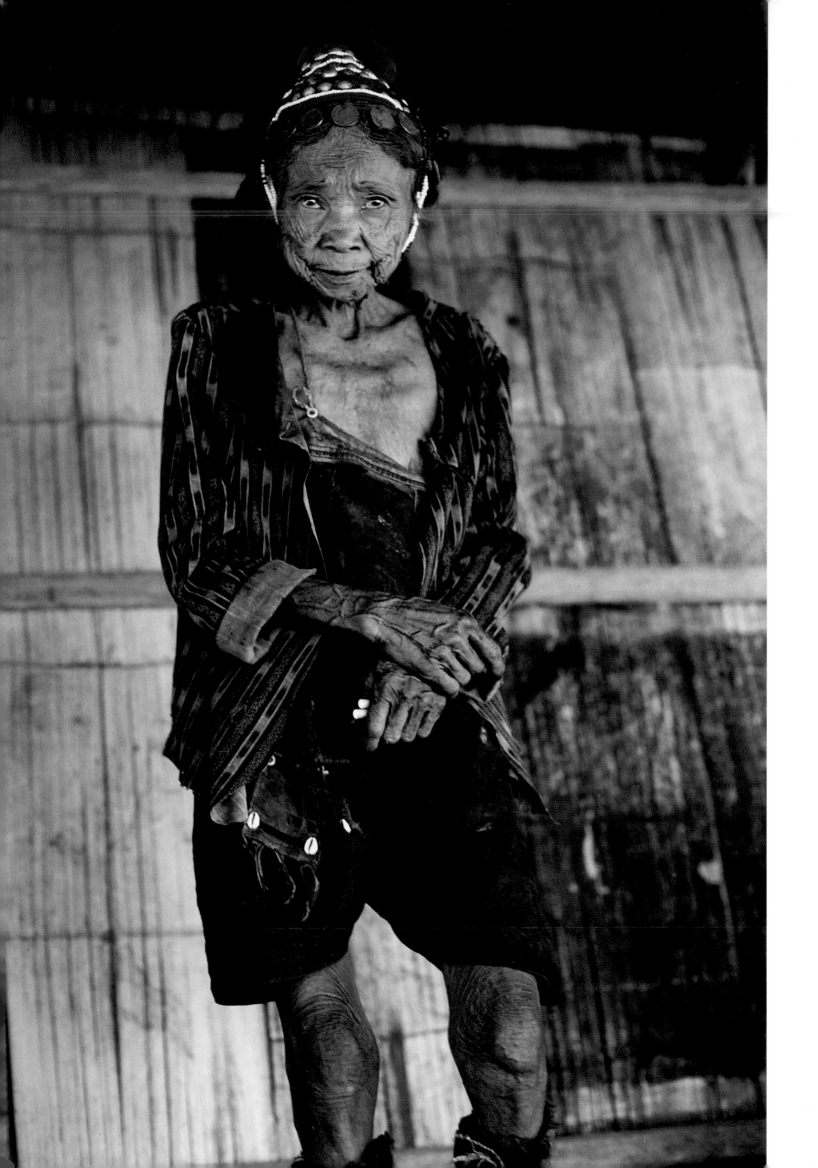

The woman opposite is at least 90 years old. She is holding two cigarettes I gave her in exchange for taking the photograph. Akha women work until they are very elderly, and then they stay at home and help look after young children. The woman above is returning from the forest, where she has collected a large basket of firewood for her family. A traditional wooden yoke across her shoulders helps spread the weight of the load. Like many Akha women, she smoked tobacco constantly. The large basket (right) with a square opening is a storage drum for rice in the village.

A young Akha girl wearing the traditional hat for unmarried girls (above, right). The more elaborate head-dress (above, left), with strings of beads and a silver necklace under the chin and a raised beaten silver panel at the back, is worn by a Loimi Akha woman in the Kengtung area of eastern Shan State. This head-dress is part of her everyday wear, as the Akhas in this region are still very traditional. Akha embroidery (opposite) is extremely intricate and includes panels of diamond and geometric shapes.

Black Lahu women in a village near the Thai–Burma border in south-east Shan State. They are wearing the striking long Lahu black robe, edged with wide white panels with red, blue, green and white stripes. The most distinctive features of their costume, however, are the enormous silver bosses, resembling shields, which are used to fasten their robes.

The Black Lahu

There are more than 100,000 Lahus in Burma, mostly around the Kengtung area. Sir J. G. Scott believed they came originally from somewhere in or near Tibet. By contrast, the Lahus themselves claim they came from much farther north and that the Chinese forced them to migrate southwards.

Many of the Lahu arrivals in Burma occurred during the nineteenth century and by the 1900s many were living in Thailand, where they are better known as *Muser* or 'hunter' on account of their skill in the chase. The war in Laos uprooted many more Lahus from their homes in the 1970s.

In Burma, the Lahus are divided into a number of related sub-groups, including the Black Lahu, or Lahu Na (pictured), and the Red Lahu, or Lahu Nyi. They are great weavers and are famed for their intricate basketwork which is much prized by other tribes. The Lahus also cultivate rice, and chilli and opium, which they smoke themselves or sell as a cash crop.

Black Lahu women and men shave the top of their heads and scrape their long hair into a top-knot, Chinese-style. Some women wear thick silver torques as well as silver bosses (above) if they can afford them. The earrings are surprisingly simple and sometimes have a single cotton thread linking them under the chin (opposite).

A Black Lahu village in the Shan borderlands. It is early morning and the old woman has risen early to fetch water in the thick bamboo containers she is carrying on her back. The gourd pipe or *ken* (opposite) is made from several gourds pierced with lengths of bamboo cane. Some Lahus believe that men and women were born from a gourd and that the sound of this instrument pleases the spirits. It is played at many Lahu ceremonies, including a full moon ceremony, when this photograph was taken.

A Red Lahu woman wearing the
elaborate blue and red jacket which is
decorated with rows and clusters of
silver beads. Like the Black Lahu, they
fasten their jackets with large silver
bosses. This woman evidently belongs
to a wealthy family as the clasps
are extremely large and finely engraved.

The Red Lahu

The Red Lahu or Lahu Nyi are very closely related to the Black
Lahu, but have slightly different dress. Unlike the Black Lahu,
Red Lahu women do not shave their heads or wear their hair in
a Chinese-style top-knot.

Spirit worshippers, the Lahus have traditionally been ruled by
messianic priest chiefs and often refer to themselves as Bon Ya,
which roughly translates as 'children of the blessing'.

Although they still believe in good and evil spirits, many
Lahus on the plains have now adopted Buddhism or were
converted to Christian beliefs by English and American Baptist
ministers who established churches in the region at the turn of
the century.

Nevertheless, in the hills, there are in existence Lahus who
retain a belief in a supreme being known as Guisha, and
millennial sects following 'man-god' prophets still occur from
time to time.

Red Lahu girls showing off their finery. Note that the woman on the left has fastened her jacket with a pin, probably because she is too poor to afford a silver boss. The girl in the centre is wearing a particularly elaborate jacket, whose central panel is edged with silver rupees. Wealthier Red Lahu women also sew silver beads and coins (including old English pennies) on the back of their jackets (below), although the main indications of wealth and status are the number and sizes of silver bosses on the costume.

Dancing is an important part of ceremonial occasions. Here, Red Lahu girls are dancing around the fire during their New Year festival in November 1996. The girls sing and stamp their feet in time to the music, forming a circle with musicians who play a gourd flute and sacred drums (below). These instruments are reserved for religious occasions and few people in the village are allowed to touch them.

An Intha girl in a boat on Lake Inle in Shan State. The Intha spend a lot of time travelling around the lake by boat, either to visit friends and relations, tend their floating allotments or sell their produce at local markets. Today Inthas are largely indistinguishable from Burmans, having adopted their dress and many of their customs.

The Intha

The name Intha is said to mean 'children of the lake', and most Intha people can be found living on or around Lake Inle in Shan State. Speaking a distinctive and unusual Burmese dialect, there is mystery over their origins in this area. Like the Pa-Os and Taungyos, it is thought that they arrived from Lower Burma many centuries ago. By one account, they are descendants of southern Burmans who migrated north during the reign of King Narapatisithu (1174–1210), although some scholars believe they stem from slaves taken captive during on-and-off wars with the Mons and Tavoyans.

The Intha are famous for their highly individual rowing technique. Fishermen wrap a paddle around one hand and leg and use this to propel the boat, while balancing precariously on the other. This position leaves them with one hand free, allowing them to drop a large conical net over passing fish in the shallow waters of the lake.

As well as hunting human skulls, the Wa use the skulls of animals to ward off evil spirits from the village, ensure that crops thrive and that the hunt is successful. This deer skull is attached to a pole in a Wa chief's house in a village north-east of Kengtung. It acts as a totem to protect the hut and the community. An older, decaying skull can be seen underneath, which has a large spider crawling along its antler.

The Wa

According to legend Wa peoples have inhabited their territory in eastern Shan State since the beginning of time. More than 100,000 Was live in Burma, and were notorious for head-hunting, which until recently they practised as part of fertility rites and religious rituals. Only twenty years ago headless corpses could be found on the road to Kengtung, and Laklai village was said to have 300 human skulls lining the road to the village.

The Was regarded the skulls they collected as a protection against evil spirits. Without a skull, they believed that their families would die and their crops fail, which would enrage their ancestors. The heads of strangers were highly prized because, the Was believed, the ghost of the dead man would be unable to find his way out of the hills.

Much of the Wa sub-state is impoverished and the mountain forests are badly denuded. Opium remains the most common cash crop, and caravans still pass through the hills.

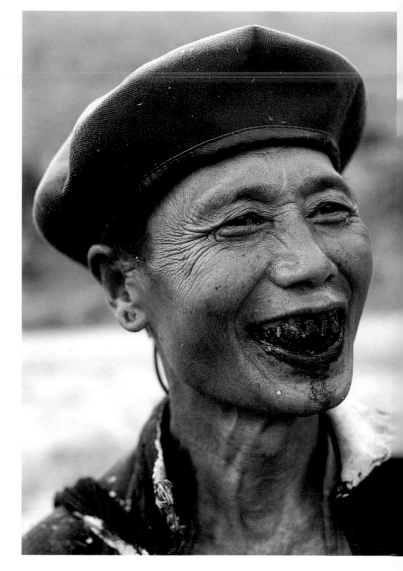

A beautiful young Wa woman wearing a black turban imaginatively decorated with beads, flowers and thread (above, left). The woman opposite has added the flowers of a palm heart to her head-dress for extra effect. Many Was – both men and women – chew betel nut, which stains the teeth black. Although they look unattractive to outsiders, black teeth are traditionally considered a sign of beauty among the Was. The man above is the village headman and consequently has a particularly impressive set.

Wa women in the eastern hills of Shan State.
When Sir J. G. Scott visited this region a century
ago, he said that in hot weather they would
go around 'all unabashed, unhaberdashed,
unheeding'. Despite the impact of war, some
villages remain largely untouched.

A young Karen woman wearing traditional silver drum earrings. The Karens would commonly pierce a child's earlobe shortly after birth and pass a small piece of thread through it to prevent the lobe healing. In the hills, some Karen children have wads of thread hanging from their ears, which stretch the lobes so that later a large silver drum can be inserted.

The Karen

Karen legends refer to a 'river of running sand' which their ancestors reputedly crossed. Many Karens think this refers to the Gobi Desert, although they have lived in Burma for centuries. Most probably, the Karen were among the earliest inhabitants to descend from China down the Irrawaddy, Sittang and Salween Rivers into Burma, but over the centuries they retreated into the mountains of the south-east and the forests of the Irrawaddy Delta under pressure from the Burmans and Mons.

If all Karen sub-groups are counted, the Karens constitute the biggest ethnic population in Burma after the Burmans and Shans. The term Karen usually refers to the major sub-groups of the Pwo and Sgaw as well as the Bwe-speakers around Toungoo. Burma is home to around 4 million Karens, half of whom live in the Delta region and the rest in the Thai borderlands. Most are Buddhists and in the eastern mountains there are still animists, but around 20 per cent have converted to Christianity.

Karen women performing daily chores. The woman pounding rice (above, right) is the village headman's wife, while the grandmother of another household is skinning a buffalo's head for the family's meal (above, left), although part of the meal will be offered as propitiation for the spirits. Karen embroidery is extremely intricate; the white grains sewn on to the blouse are not rice but seeds called 'Job's tears'.

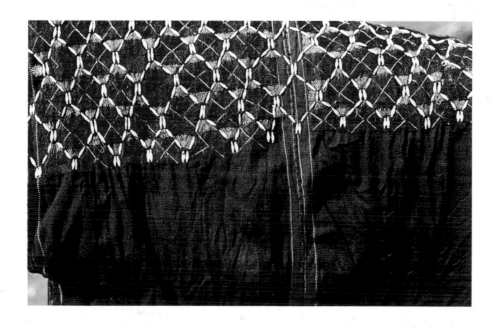

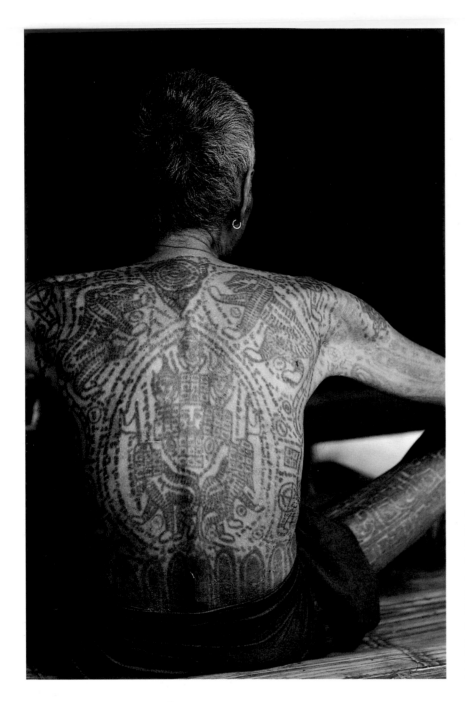

Young and old Karen villagers. The tattooed man (left) was the father of the Karen guide who took me to Lisu villages in Burma. Historically, tattoos were very significant for Karen men as they were an indication of a man's strength and endurance. At one time, no Karen woman would ever consider a man who was not tattooed for a husband, although the custom has fallen out of favour in recent years. The designs are of magical symbols which the Karens believe will ward off harm; the face and hands are never tattooed. Note the red tattoo underneath the blue-black ink.

A Kayah woman wearing the traditional red striped shawl from which Karennis derived the name of 'Red Karens'. She is also wearing the distinctive silver pendant earrings, coil bracelets and lacquered cotton leg rings.

The Kayah

The Kayah are the largest ethnic group in Kayah State. It was from their brightly coloured head-cloths or shawls that the territory gained its historic name of Karenni – or 'Red Karen' – which today applies to all the Karen sub-groups in the state.

Although numerically smaller, the Kayah represent one of the four major linguistic branches of the Karens – together with the Pwo, Sgaw and Pa-O. In 1951 Karenni State, which had gained the right of secession under the 1948 constitution, was renamed Kayah State by the government, with the intention, some historians say, of making a divisive distinction between Karennis and Karens, both of whom had been fighting for independence. Although animism is still practised, many Kayahs – like other Karennis – have converted to Christianity over the past century.

The name given to Kayah women by the Burmans is 'elephant women', because of the numerous lacquered cotton rings they wear below the knee.

Kayah women in traditional dress. The red striped shawl was originally a head-cloth which was adapted to wear around the shoulders (left and opposite). A simple black tunic is worn which is tied with a broad white sash decorated with coloured tassles. Rich Karenni women wear silver coin necklaces and silver earrings, bracelets and leg rings. Lacquered cotton leg rings have largely replaced silver leg rings, although these women are still wearing a couple each. The rings make walking very difficult; when sitting, the women must stretch out their legs as they cannot bend them, and circulation in the lower leg and feet can be affected (left and below).

These Karenni women have adapted the traditional
costume into a stylish dress. The two who are
not wearing head-dresses have just returned from the
fields and with heavy loads on their heads. Older
women can be seen wearing traditional heavy earrings
and jewellery (above), even when working in the fields.

A Bre man in traditional costume. Although Bre women wear far more jewellery, most men wear silver bracelets, necklaces, earrings and leg rings. He is also wearing lacquered cotton rings around his neck and legs, which are similar to those of Karenni women.

The Bre

Very little is known about the origins of the Bre, who are a small Karen sub-group in the Karenni area. The term is often used to refer to two closely related groups, the Kayaw and the Minoo-Minaw. Indeed, the sheer diversity of Karen peoples in this region has led some scholars to suggest that the remote mountains around the western Karenni borders were the original Karen *heimat*, where Karen cultures diversified and evolved. Many Bres prefer to remain deep in the hills, and this cautious behaviour is thought to stem from a time in their history when slave-raiding by outside peoples was commonplace.

Bre territory, like much of the Kayah State, has suffered badly in recent warfare. In order to photograph these Bres, I sent a truck into Kayah State to bring them to me in Shan State. A Bre friend escorted them and managed to allay their fears. I was astonished that they looked exactly like the photographs of them that I had seen in the March 1922 issue of *National Geographic*.

Bre jewellery is among the most beautiful of all Burma's hill peoples' adornments. Many necklaces are worn (opposite), made from shells, beads and brass coils, and fashioned from silver. Distended earlobes are plugged with rings of silver (above, left) and the ankles and knees are encased with brass coils, sometimes decorated with a line of jingling bells (above, right). Old Indian rupees and British coins from colonial days adorn silver pendants (below).

The Padaung

The Padaung are found in a 150-square-mile area of Kayah State and Shan State, west of the Salween river and around the Pekon hills, which rise to 5,000 feet. For centuries they have been objects of curiosity and were once brought to the palace of the King of Mandalay for inspection. They are part of the Kayan sub-group of Karens. Although known in the world as Padaung, they call themselves Ka-Kaung, which means 'people who live on top of the hill'. In recent years, many have become Catholics.

The Padaungs are often nicknamed 'giraffe women' or the 'long-necked Karens' because of the custom of encasing the neck in brass coils. The practice is fast disappearing, and today can only be found in a few villages. When a girl is aged between five and nine, her neck is rubbed with ointment said to be made of dog fat, coconut milk and royal jelly, and the first neck ring is fitted. After two years, the next set of coils is added and every year thereafter she gains a new set until she marries.

It is not unusual for girls as young as twelve to have a full set of neck coils (left); note, too, the ring at the base of her neck, which some people thought was once used to chain up Padaung women in times of raids. Below the chin they wear a square cotton pad decorated with beads and pom-poms, which prevents chafing (opposite). The heavy silver jewellery is only worn in villages, as Padaung women would be afraid of thieves outside their areas. This jewellery (below) is known as flowered silver because of its pattern, and some of the pieces are centuries old.

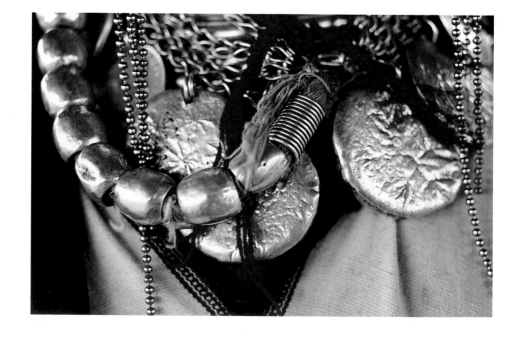

This Padaung woman (opposite) is wearing an unusual turban made of towels, scarves and cotton thread twisted into a unique style. As well as neck coils, Padaung women have two sets of leg rings, one above the knee and one below, but this does not seem to hamper them as they go about their daily chores in the fields (right) and villages. Little girls have their first set of neck rings fitted early, some as young as five (below).

The Lahta

The Lahta or Zayein live in rugged pine-forested country, 30 miles west of Pekon and Pinlaung, along the northern Kayah State border with the Shan State. A guerrilla war between different Karenni forces, the Pa-O National Organisation and the Burmese government, has closed off the area in which the Lahta live, so they agreed to meet me outside their home territory. I had to climb for fourteen miles over forested hills of 6,000 feet in order to meet them.

Lahtas wear white smocks or jackets over striped red skirts or short longyi, and red and white conical hats. Women wear traditional brass coils from the wrist to the elbow, making arm movements difficult. Food has to be tossed into the mouth as the forearms cannot bend.

Every Lahta village has an elder or spirit master on whom the villagers rely for advice on when to marry, to mount hunting expeditions or to sow their crops.

Lahta dress consists of a Chinese-style white jacket edged in red and a short white longyi for the men, and a white smock and red-and-white striped longyi for the women. Both sexes wear a conical white hat edged in red, lacquered cotton leg rings, many strings of beads and earrings of coloured thread. The iridescent green objects dangling from the earrings (below) are beetle wings. Some women also wear arm rings which stretch from the elbow to the forearm, although this custom is dying out as it is difficult to eat when the arm cannot bend. Some women have started to wear woollen sleeves with coloured bands which recall the brass coils (opposite).

A young Yinbaw girl from Kayah State. Her simple black dress and headscarf are set off with necklaces of old Burmese and British colonial coins, cowry shells, beads and rows of colourful cotton pom-poms. She has also attached several lengths of cotton thread to her simple silver earrings.

The Yinbaw

The Yinbaw are ethnic Karens of the Kayan sub-group; however, politically they are usually regarded as Karennis. They mostly live in the plains areas of Kantarawaddy and Bawlakhe in Kayah State. Indeed, they call themselves the Kang-ngan, which means 'plain-dwellers' in the Karen language. Almost nothing else has been recorded about them in historical texts.

Like other Karens, the Yinbaws were traditionally animists, but many willingly converted to Christianity during the nineteenth century with the arrival of American Baptist missionaries in Kayah State. Once a year between March and May the Yinbaws celebrate a traditional pole-raising festival called Kathowbow, when these photographs were taken. The object of the festival is to ensure good luck and prevent famine or illness in the coming year. This custom is also practised by the Kayahs, Bres and Kayans, although in many villages it has often been disrupted by continuing outbreaks of fighting with government forces.

It is difficult to say whether Yinbaw men or women have the more beautiful costume. Both wear short longyis covered with colourful pom-poms, and similarly decorated head-dresses. However, whereas the women's costume is mainly black, the men wear a blue-and-white striped smock, white headscarf and a single lacquered cotton leg ring. Although he looks extremely stern, the man opposite burst into peals of laughter seconds after this photograph was taken.

Kyaiktiyo Pagoda is, along with Pagan and the Shwedagon, one of country's most wondrous sites. A small stupa is perched on top of the gargantuan 'Golden Rock', a huge boulder covered in gold leaf which balances precariously on the edge of a cliff at the top of Mt Kyaikto. At dawn, as pilgrims light incense and fires around its base, the huge golden dome shimmers in the early morning light, catching the first rays of sunshine.

The Mon

A distinctive branch of the Mon-Khmer peoples, the Mon were probably the earliest of modern-day inhabitants to settle in the plains of Burma. They soon established themselves as the most cultured people in South-east Asia at that time, as their art and architecture clearly show. The Mons brought both Buddhism and writing to Burma and traded with India as early as the Christian era. The earliest Mon writings date from the fifth century AD, and they are believed to have founded the world-famous Shwedagon Pagoda in Rangoon, originally a Mon settlement.

For a thousand years, until the fall of Pegu in 1757, the Mons ruled much of Lower Burma from their great cities at Thaton, Martaban and Pegu. Many Mons believe that the whole of South-east Asia could have come under their control had their forefathers been a race of warriors rather than artists and poets.

Mon State is home to the Kyaiktiyo Pagoda, an extraordinary golden rock perched precariously on a mountain outcrop.

Legend has it that the Kyaiktiyo rock is balanced on a single hair of the Buddha and will remain perfectly poised for ever. Today, thousands of pilgrims visit the rock and marvel at its size and precariousness. Women are not allowed to touch it, but a small boy could rock the boulder like a toy with the merest whisper of a touch. The sound of the boulder rocking is indescribably deep and resonant – the sound of creation at its most primeval.

Mon girls in Mon State, close to the Thai border. Although the Mons were once the dominant group in the region, today many have assimilated Burman dress and customs. Red-coloured longyis remain popular among both men and women. Today, traditional Mon language and culture survive mostly in rural areas and the south-east borderlands.

This Thet (or Shakama) woman from the Kaladan River region in Arakan State broke down and cried after I photographed her, amazed that anyone would be interested in her people today. In 1919, C. C. Lowis said the Thet were practically disappearing from Arakan State, remarking that only 230 villagers had returned themselves as Thet in the census of 1901.

Arakan State

The Rakhine, who are the majority ethnic group in Arakan State, have long been influenced by their proximity to India and have formed strong trading links with the sub-continent. They claim a long history of independence and ruled their own kingdom at Mrauk-U (Myohaung) until 1784 AD.

The recorded names of kings and imprint of Buddhism date back to the early centuries AD, but it is not certain whether this refers to the same people. Buddhism was reputedly established during the reign of King Chandra Surya in 146 AD, and most Rakhines are still devout Buddhists today.

The Rakhines speak a dialect of Burmese that many scholars believe is the earliest form of the language, and in culture and dress they are very similar to Burmans. About one-quarter of Arakan's population are Muslims known as Rohingyas, mostly of Bengali descent, and other minority groups include the Thet, Khami, Daignet and Maramagyi, who live in the hills.

A Khami (or Mro) woman from Mrauk-U in Arakan State. The tattoos on her shoulders are an extremely rare sight today (right). In the old days, every Khami woman tattooed her shoulders to complement the tribe's exquisite weaving; Khami cloth is so fine that one panel of a dress can take six months to complete and the weave is said to be so tight that it is waterproof. Note the panel (below) which has cleverly incorporated the first three letters of the Western alphabet into the design.

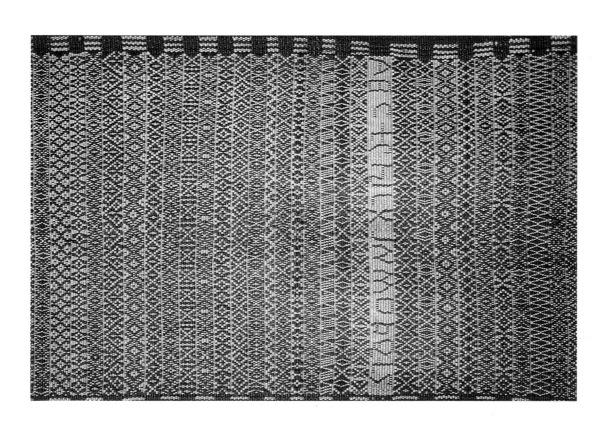

A Daignet man (opposite) in traditional costume. This man was head of a village on the Lemro River in Arakan State and the only one to possess a traditional Daignet robe. The Maramagyi girl (above, left) is carrying water from a river between the Kaladan and Lemro Rivers, while the Rakhine girl (above, right) is practising the skilful art of washing while fully clothed in her sarong.

A Chin Bon woman from Kanpetlet in the Pakokku Hills of Chin State. Chin Bon is one of the southern Chin clans, along with the Chin Bok and Laytoo, which are distinguished by different facial tattoos. Chin Bon tattoos consist of a series of dots and lines.

The Chin

The Chin, or Zomi, are a Tibeto-Burman people who inhabit the great mountain chain running up western Burma into Mizoram in north-east India. In previous centuries, the difficult terrain meant that there was little communication between villages, and the Chins had to rely on their lowland neighbours for food and supplies in times of emergency.

More than forty sub-groups, many distinguished by their unique facial tattoos and costumes, have been identified among the 1.5 million Chins in Burma. According to folklore, the custom of tattooing originated almost a thousand years ago, after Burman men found the Chin women so attractive that they would capture them in slave raids. In their fear, the women began to tattoo their faces – both to make themselves look unattractive, and to ensure that Chin men would be able to identify them if they were carried off.

Close up, the tattooed faces of Chin women resemble strange, exotic birds (opposite). Young girls are tattooed at a young age and as they grow the design stretches across their faces, creating very individual features. Chin men, however, are not tattooed; this Chin Bon village headman (left) is resplendent in his ceremonial silk head-dress decorated with rooster feathers and strings of cowry shells, and has thick discs of gold in his ears (below).

Laytoo Chin men and women from southern Chin State. This clan of Chin sport unusual facial tattoos which closely resemble a spider's web or a sunrise (above). The woman opposite comes from a different village even though she is tattooed in the same way. She was the only Laytoo Chin woman I saw wearing traditional drum-shaped silver earrings. Note that the Laytoo Chin archer (left) is wearing the same earrings as his Chin Bon kinsman (p. 168).

A Naga warrior in traditional dress
from Singkaling Hkamti on the
Chindwin River near the Indian border.
His magnificent head-dress consists
of a rattan hat topped with black
monkey fur and long hornbill feathers.
Two wild boars' tusks frame his face,
and a string of tiger claws forms
a chin-strap. Two white tigers' teeth
hang from his necklace, a sign of
his prowess as a hunter.

The Naga

The name Naga embraces a number of Indo-Mongoloid tribes who speak a distant Tibeto-Burman language and live in the mountain regions of the India–Burma border. Around one million Nagas live in India, although some 100,000 inhabit the Patkai range in northern Burma. Traditionally fierce warriors and, until recently, head-hunters, the Nagas have defended their land against incursions by Indian and Burmese government troops.

Unlike the Was, who took human skulls to safeguard their society and crops, the Nagas killed for personal glory and for the glory of their villages. The practice of head-hunting is believed to have died out in the past twenty years. Although Nagas would not buy skulls like the Was sometimes did, slaves were bought to be decapitated for their skulls and their heads were hung in baskets high in bamboo groves with arrows driven through the eye sockets, to ensure that the ghost would protect the village.

A Naga elder (opposite) and young warrior (above). The elder is wearing two large white shells over his ears, a sign of great wealth and standing; being so distant from the coast, shells were historically used by hill peoples as a form of currency and are still highly prized by many ethnic groups in Burma.

These photographs were taken during the Naga New Year celebrations in 1996. Men and women from many different Naga groups had poured into the town of Singkaling Hkamti on the Chindwin River, a few miles' walk from the Indian border. Although it is a time for celebration, the Nagas pictured are wearing their everyday dress (opposite and right). Young Naga men would be expected to stay in a bachelors' house – or *morung* – which is decorated with carved snakes or animals (above). Naga warriors are eager to show off their hunting prowess; the sight and sound of twenty armed warriors performing a war dance is fearsome.

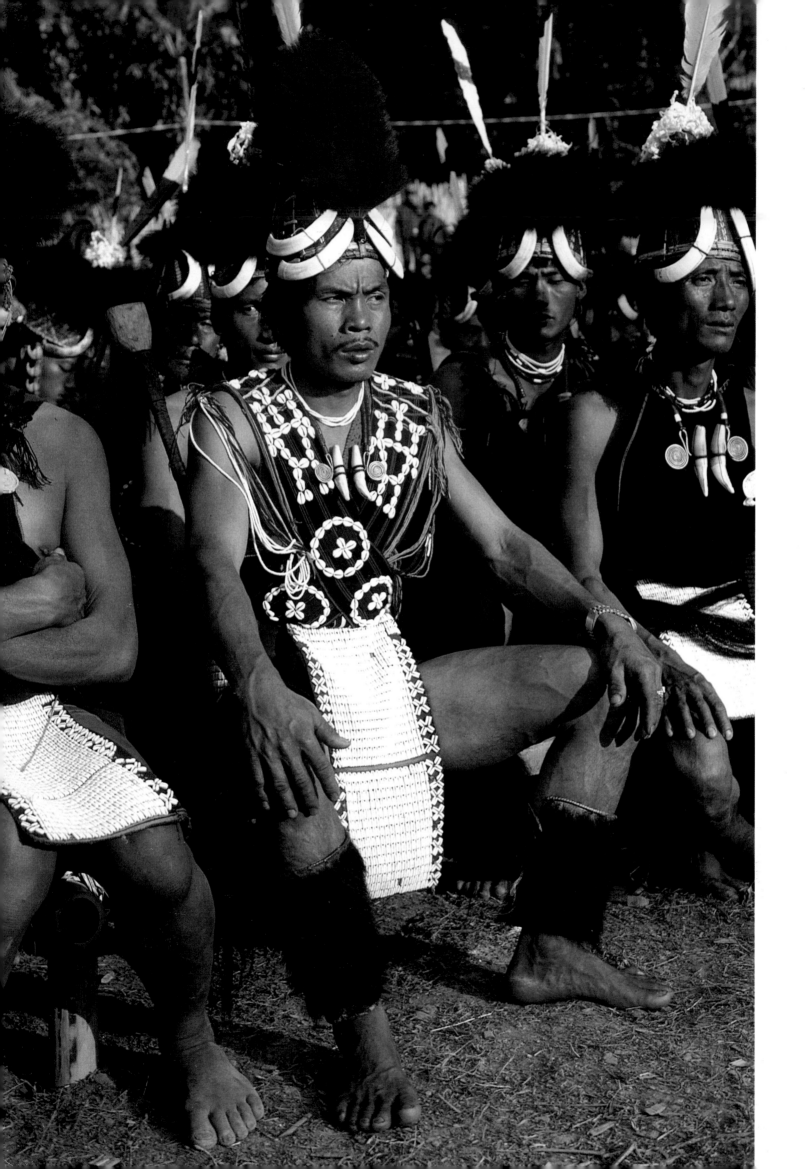

A Naga chief (opposite) sits with his warriors for an official ceremony. He is distinguished by the dyed red monkey fur plume on his head-dress and the vast array of cowry shells adorning his costume and sash, a sign of great wealth in the clan. The fledgling warriors (right) are from a different clan; their head-dresses sport more hornbill feathers and their sashes are decorated with large brass plates. The woven rattan armband (below) is used by archers to protect their arms in case their bow-strings snap.

While Naga warriors show off their prowess, unmarried Naga women dress in their finest clothes in the hope of attracting a husband. These young woman are around eighteen years old; traditionally, if they met a man they liked at the celebration, they would be able to disappear into the forest to make love without incurring the anger of their parents. In recent years, however, many Nagas have become Christians and such practices are discouraged.

The Burman

The upper and central plains of Burma are the traditional home of the Burman, a Tibeto-Burman people who migrated from the north and China–India borderlands up until the eleventh century AD. The Burmans (or Bamas or Myanmas) established their greatest capital at Pagan between 1044 and 1287 AD on the banks of the Irrawaddy. Later capitals were built at Ava, Amarapura, Sagaing, Mandalay and Toungoo.

Today, Burmans form the largest ethnic group in the country, with 30 million people – about 60 per cent of the population – speaking only their language, Burmese. In the past century, many minority groups, especially Mons and Karens, have become assimilated as Burman migrants spread into new areas.

Like the Mons, the rich culture of the Burmans, who are strongly Buddhist, shows influences of Indian civilisations. These include Pali script (derived from Sanskrit), cosmology, philosophy and statecraft, art, medicine and architecture.

A *Shin Byu* procession in central Burma (opposite). An ethnic Burman boy, like all Buddhists in Burma, is not considered a good Buddhist until he has gone through this initiation rite, which involves him dressing up as the Prince Siddhartha Gautama (who became the Buddha) and riding to the monastery, where his head is shaved, he takes on the robes of a monk and he lives in the monastery to receive instruction. Most Burman festivals are Buddhist in origin, although some reflect spirit worship which pre-dates Theravada Buddhism. *Nat* festivals – or *Nat-pwe* – are a case in point; many of the country's Buddhist inhabitants still worship the thirty-seven *Nats*, who are the spirits of legendary heroes, at the annual *Nat-pwe* festival during the Burmese month of Nayon (May to June). The principal performer at the *Nat-pwe* is the *Nat-kadaw* or 'spirit wife' (above), who falls into a mediumistic trance and dances wildly in front of the crowd; she (or he) would then offer advice of a spiritual nature, or healing.

A brass statue of the Buddha (overleaf) in the Sule Pagoda, Rangoon. Note the elongated ears: all images of the Buddha have these, because Gautama was said to have had long ears. The coloured rings in the background are neon lights which illuminate the image after dark. Like the Shwedagon Pagoda, the Sule Pagoda is said to house legendary hairs of the Buddha, although it takes its name from the Sule *Nat*, guardian spirit of Rangoon's Singuttara Hill.

Dhammayangyi Pagoda (left) was built by King Narathu in the mid-twelfth century and is the largest of the pagodas found on the plains of Pagan. The so-called city of 'four million temples' on the banks of the Irrawaddy River was founded in the mid-ninth century by the Burmans and was their most glorious capital until it was sacked by Kublai Khan and his Mongol armies in 1287. Today, the ancient city is uninhabited and the remnants of thousands of temples, *Nat* shrines and pagodas stand alone across the arid plains. The reclining Buddha (below) is a common pose, representing the Buddha's attainment of nirvana.

Mount Popa (above) is an old volcano whose outer casing of soil has been washed away, exposing the rock core which rises 1,500 feet above the plains outside Pagan. Traditionally, every Burman king would make a pilgrimage to Mount Popa, the legendary home of the *Nats* or spirits, to consult them before his reign could begin. Pilgrims visit Mount Popa in the Burmese month of Nayon (May to June) to celebrate the annual festival of spirits. Of the thirty-seven *Nats*, the two most revered are the Mahagiri *Nats* who live in Mount Popa. Legend has it that they were a brother and sister who lived in the sixth century; the brother was reputedly burned alive in a flowering jasmine tree by the king, and his grief-stricken sister, the king's wife, threw herself into the same fire.

Burman marionette theatre – or *yok-thei pwe* – was developed during the reign of King Bagyidaw in the early nineteenth century and was the forerunner of live theatre (opposite). There are still a few master puppeteers in Burma, but the skill is dying out and efforts have been made to train youngsters in the art; this puppeteer is a seventeen-year-old girl from Pagan. People still visit the marionette theatre, however, and know all the characters; this puppet is Taw Bilu, or the jungle ogre, whose dance is a show of evil power and strength, accompanied by foreboding music. Burmese lacquerware (above) is painstakingly painted; originally from China, Burma's earliest known surviving piece of lacquerware dates from 1274.

A Burman dancer from Myawaddy near the Thai border town of Mae Sot (opposite). Burman classical music and dance was reputedly adopted from Thai prisoners under King Hsinbyushin, although there is an older stratum of vocal folk music which survives in court dances. Although the young girl above appears to have lost all vestiges of traditional culture, her elaborately coiled hair may well be an echo of her people's Tibeto-Burman origins.

Ethnographical History

Gillian Cribbs with Martin Smith

MUCH of Burma's complex ethnic history remains shrouded in mystery. The present political map, under the 1974 constitution, demarcates seven ethnic minority states for the largest non-Burman nationality groups – the Chin, Kachin, Karen, Kayah (Karenni), Mon, Rakhine and Shan. In fact, more than 100 different languages and dialects have been identified in the country. Modern anthropologists, however, are agreed that virtually all of Burma's diverse sub-groups and peoples are descended from just four major ethnic families: the Mon-Khmer, Tibeto-Burman, Tai (Shan) and Karen, the last of which is often considered a distant sub-group of Tibeto-Burman.

Burma absorbed many waves of migrations in its early history, while original inhabitants, such as the Pyu, simply disappeared. Most of the new migrants came from the north and followed the lines of least geographical resistance – along hill ridges and river courses.

First came the Mon-Khmer, who are today represented by the Buddhist Mons of Lower Burma and their remote hill cousins, the Was and Palaungs in Shan State. Next probably came ancestors of the Karens and Chins. The first Burmans and related Burmese speakers, such as the Rakhines, may also have appeared in the early centuries AD, before the main body of Burman migration began descending from the north, probably around the ninth and tenth centuries. Burman settlers occupied the upper reaches of the Irrawaddy River, before going on to establish their great kingdoms at Pagan and later capitals at Toungoo, Ava, Amarapura and Mandalay.

Around the same time, ethnic Shans (Tais) began crossing the mountains from Yunnan province in south-west China, and by the thirteenth century they had established beach-heads across north-east Burma. Finally came another wave of Tibeto-Burman hill peoples, including the Lahus, Akhas and various sub-groups of the Kachins.

Until the British annexation of Burma in the 1800s, there followed centuries of warfare as political power constantly ebbed and flowed between the valley or city-state kingdoms, which were dominated by Burman, Mon, Rakhine and Shan rulers. In the mountains the different hill peoples continued to resist slave-raiding or any military incursions. Cultural and political values, however, were constantly exchanged between the different ethnic groups.

The result was the complicated ethnic mosaic which makes up Burma today, where few regions are truly ethnically exclusive and shared linguistic or cultural traditions have metamorphosed into many different forms. Of the Tibeto-Burman peoples, for example, the plains-dwelling Rakhines and Tavoyans speak a dialect which is close to the Burman majority, while hill peoples, such as the Chins, Kachins and Lahus, have developed distinctive cultures which also display many variant forms.

Following the final Anglo-Burmese war of 1885–6, the British instituted a two-tier administration system to govern the vast territories which they had annexed as a new province of the Indian Empire. A political distinction was made between the quasi-parliamentary 'Ministerial Burma' – the central plains of Burma Proper where the Burman majority live – and the ethnic minority 'Frontier Areas', where local administration remained under the traditional rulers and headmen.

On the eve of the British annexation, for example, Shan territory consisted of thirty-three sub-states ruled by *sawbwas*, or feudal princes, assisted by village headmen who controlled the civil, criminal and fiscal affairs of the region. The British thus introduced a dual system whereby the *sawbwas* ruled alongside colonial officers, who set up administrative centres in important provincial

HKAHKU WITH SHIELD
Hkahku people mostly live in Kachin State in the area of the Mali Hka and N'Mai Hka Rivers.

James Henry Green Collection, 1920s

CHINGHPAW PRIEST
Chinghpaw and Singhpo were early
British names for the Jinghpaw, the
majority group among the Kachins.

James Henry Green Collection, 1920s

towns such as Taunggyi, Maymyo, Kalaw, Lashio
and Kutkai.

The 'Pax Britannica', however, did not mark an
end to the historic flow of peoples through the
country. Local villagers believe that the Shans
halted the southwards migration of the Jinghpaws,
who in turn moved into areas inhabited by
Palaungs. Lahus were on the move in the late
nineteenth century and Lisus flowed into Mogok
in the 1900s. Akhas, Lisus and others continued
to move south, with the first clans reaching
Thailand in the 1920s.

The subsequent destruction and bloodshed of the
Second World War simply added to this process.
Such movements have continued until today. In
1949, following the communist victory in China,
thousands of Chinese Kuomintang soldiers fled
from Yunnan province into Shan State, where

many scattered into the mountains before settling.
The greatest movements, however, have occurred
among the indigenous peoples within Burma itself.

The tasks of political integration facing Burma
at independence in 1948 were enormous, and
they have never been resolved. Countrywide
insurrections broke out shortly afterwards that
came to involve ethnic groups as diverse as the
Karen, Mon, Karenni, Pa-O, Rakhine, Shan,
Kachin, Chin, Kayan, Naga, Lahu, Rohingya
Muslims, Palaung and Wa, and all these struggles
have continued into the 1990s. Ethnic Burmans
have also taken up arms. After decades of ethnic
and political violence, the loss of life and internal
displacement have been massive.

As a result, many unique cultures are in danger of
disappearing. Within our time, small minority

SINGHPO GIRL
Jinghpaw has become the lingua
franca among the Kachin peoples,
who call themselves Wunpawng.

James Henry Green Collection, 1920s

groups, notably among the Karen and Wa, have vanished completely or have been absorbed by larger groups like the Danu, who in turn have been gradually absorbed by Burmans or Shans.

Across the country, entire communities have become militarised. Army checkpoints dot the roads and hillsides, and hundreds of thousands of minority villagers have been ordered to relocate to government-controlled areas on the plains under counter-insurgency operations such as the 'Four Cuts'. In response, many inhabitants have fled into neighbouring countries. Currently, there are more than half a million refugees and illegal migrants (predominantly Karens, Karennis, Mons and Shans) in Thailand and tens of thousands of minority Muslim refugees in Bangladesh, as well as Chins in India.

As a result of such upheavals, today there are no reliable statistics on, or breakdown of, Burma's different ethnic populations. An estimated two-thirds of Burma's 48 million inhabitants are Burmans or related Burmese speakers such as the Rakhines, and the remaining population is divided into six or seven main minority groups, each with its own language, sub-groups or cultures.

The most sizeable ethnic minorities are the Shans and Karens (around 8–10 per cent each); the Mons (3 per cent), the Chins and Kachins (2–3 per cent), and the related Palaungs and Was (1 per cent), although these figures are only rough estimates. There are also sizeable minorities of Indian and Chinese extraction in many parts of the country.

There has been an increase in settlement on the plains or in growing conurbations over the years, and this has affected all ethnic groups. Most Mon and Rakhine farmers, for example, practise wet-rice cultivation as do the majority of Burmans. But in the hills, many minority communities still practise a shifting cultivation – burning a small area of the forest or

jungle and planting rice, corn and other crops for a few years. When the soil is exhausted, they abandon the land until the vegetation replenishes it. Some groups shift fields in a ten to fifteen year rotation, while others move entire villages. To obtain salt, metal implements, and other goods not found in the forests, they trade agricultural and forest produce at markets. In north-east Burma, the best places to see a variety of such hill peoples are at the regional Shan markets, which rotate over a five-day period – beginning, for example, in Heho, thence to Taunggyi, westto Kalaw and finally to Pindaya, north-west of Inle Lake.

Even finding common words to describe such a rich admixture of peoples is a challenge which frequently defies outside writers. Terms such as 'races', 'ethnic groups', 'nationalities', 'indigenous peoples' and 'tribes' have tended to come in and out of fashion. This book concentrates, in the main, on the anthropological influences or cultures that, in British days, were considered 'traditional' or 'tribal'. However, although Burma has long been known as an anthropologist's paradise, there have been virtually no new studies conducted in the field since the pioneering works of Edmund Leach in the early 1950s.

The ethnic groups featured in this book, therefore, have been arranged according to the states or territories in which they were photographed. This was the most logical way of presenting them, as there is no universally agreed classification system for all of Burma's different nationalities and sub-groups. Although many scholars rely on language for classification, it is not a conclusive

VILLAGERS ON THE RIVER BANK
In the Kachin Hills, as elsewhere
in Burma, the rivers are the natural
thoroughfares of the region.

James Henry Green Collection, 1920s

NUNG GIRL SMOKING DUNHILL PIPE
The Nung people live in the far north
of the country near the borders with
India and China.

James Henry Green Collection, 1920s

test because many peoples have absorbed the speech of their neighbours – and in some cases have abandoned their own languages completely.

Some ethnic minorities form large groups and maintain contacts across national borders, while smaller groups survive in isolated pockets or have become assimilated into larger groups. Some of the distinctions in Kachin State, where different sub-groups often live in close proximity, are even more confusing. The Nung-Rawangs of the north near Putao speak many variations of language, which gradually merge with the language of the Marus to the south; Lashi is a dialect of Maru; while Azi falls between Maru and Jinghpaw.

Nor is costume a reliable guide to classification, although each ethnic group has some distinctive clothing, particularly for women. Some groups, like the Palaung and Akha, distinguish between married and unmarried women. Wearing a costume is a declaration of belonging to an ethnic grouping or individual clan, although this can change through marriage. A Wa woman marrying into a Shan family would soon dress and speak as a Shan. Men's costumes have changed more quickly because they are more often engaged in trade and commerce, which entails greater travelling, while women care for the needs of the village, family and household.

Given these considerations, it is remarkable that Burma's different ethnic groups have managed to retain so much of their linguistic, cultural and artistic heritage until the end of the twentieth century and the dawn of the twenty-first. As these photographs, taken from the Sir James George Scott and Colonel James Henry Green collections, clearly show, little has really changed in the last century. By documenting Burma's ethnic groups, Richard Diran has not only contributed to the anthropological study of the country, but has also raised our awareness and understanding of these proud and dignified peoples.

KACHIN STATE

Kachin State is the northernmost region of Burma, bordering India to the north-west, Tibet to the far north and China to the east. Burma's highest mountain, the Hkakabo Razi (19,294 feet) near the border with Tibet, is in Kachin State. Even under British rule, much of Kachin State was not penetrated for many years because it bordered on autonomous tribal regions in India and remote parts of China.

After 1961, the thirty-three year civil war in Kachin State took a heavy toll on all ethnic communities: many of the Jinghpaws, Marus and other sub-groups were driven from their villages or were conscripted as porters and later perished in the fighting. Civilian casualties alone are estimated at over 30,000. However, following the 1994 ceasefire between the Kachin Independence Organisation (KIO) and the central Burmese government, the state has begun to open up and villagers have started to return to their former homes.

The ethnic name Kachin appears to have originated as a general name given by their lowland neighbours to the local hill peoples of Tibeto-Burman origin who call themselves Wunpawng. Now, however, it is widely accepted by speakers of all the Kachin dialects, who originally migrated from Yunnan province in south-west China and occupy the great tract of hill-country in northern Burma around the headwaters of the Chindwin and Irrawaddy rivers. Ethnic Kachins also live in north-east India and China, and have spread into the northern Shan State, where more than 100,000 also live today. Generally, it is thought that the Kachins were among the last of the Tibeto-Burman peoples to migrate into the country.

By the time of the last British census in 1931, Kachins constituted about half the population of the territory now incorporated into Kachin State. The predominant sub-groups are the *Jinghpaw* and their close relations, the *Hkahku*. The name Hkahku means 'up river (people)', and they live mainly in the northern triangle area around Sumprabum and the Mali Hka River. The Jinghpaws, by contrast, migrated more widely, spreading southwards along the Chindwin and Irrawaddy Rivers.

The next major sub-group are the *Maru* and the closely-related *Lashi* and *Azi*, whose cultures are often indistinguishable from the Jinghpaw and who also often speak the Jinghpaw dialect. This has become the lingua franca for most of Burma's estimated 1.5 million Kachins. Although widely distributed, most Marus and Lashis can be found in the China-Burma borderlands, especially in and around the Triangle and N'Mai Hka valley areas.

A third – and smaller – sub-group of Kachins are the *Nung* and *Rawang*, collectively called the Nung-Rawangs, who live in the far north around Putao. Best known for the crossbow hunting skills of the Rawangs, very few studies have ever been conducted on these remote peoples.

Finally, the last ethnic group included locally with the Kachins are the *Lisu*. Elsewhere in the region, Lisus are usually classified with other ethnic groups or alone, but in the Kachin State their language and cultures have become more integrated with the Kachins.

Under the British, many Kachins joined the British army, and large numbers also converted to Christianity. Today the majority of Kachins are Baptists, with substantial communities of Catholics in some areas. The resultant changes of the last century have seen a dynamic pan-Kachin nationalism emerge, and many families and villagers have long since settled in the valleys and towns.

In the mountains, however, there are still areas where ancient spirit worship and agricultural practices survive. Like most Kachins, the Jinghpaws traditionally built their villages on mountain ridges. Most villages would be entered through a sacred grove or *numshang* marked by prayer posts. Here, villagers would make sacrifices in dedicated shrines to propitiate *Nats* or spirits, especially the Earth spirit.

FIVE NUNG BOYS
Hunting has traditionally been important to the Nung, who are closely related to the Rawang.

James Henry Green Collection, 1920s

Traditionally, the Kachins are mainly farmers, cultivating rice, maize, tobacco, vegetables and – on occasion – opium, which they use as a medium of exchange for salt and other necessities. In some areas, especially in Shan State, they have adopted wet-rice cultivation along the valley floors. They also rear domestic animals and supplement their diets with fish and game hunted during the cold season from December to February. Men clear and burn the forest plantation areas, while women are responsible for tending, harvesting and threshing the crops. They also fetch water and firewood, weave cloth and make clothes.

TWO MARU GIRLS
The Maru are the second major
Kachin sub-group and live in the
China borderlands.

James Henry Green Collection, 1920s

Somewhat uniquely, Kachin societies were
historically divided into two systems, either
gumsa (aristocratic) or *gumlao* (democratic).
Each had its own rules for marriage, law and
religion, although both forms included chiefs and
commoners and were subject to change. A slave
or serf system also existed until this century, but
like the practice of *gumsa-gumlao* this has been
abolished or encouraged to die out.

Still surviving, however, are elaborate clan
systems, which transcend both ethnic sub-groups
and the recent adoption by many Kachins of
Christianity. The British originally mistook such
clans for ethnic sub-groups. In fact, there are still
five major clans – the Marip, Lahpai, Lahtaw,
N'hKum and Maran – with an evolving variety
of minor branches and groups. All Kachin chiefs
trace descent back to Ninggawn Wa, an original
Creator, but membership of a clan denotes kinship

and familial relations – and even whom one may
or may not marry. Marriage is mostly by
arrangement and the bride price traditionally
assessed by the standing of the bride, although
the bridegroom is often obliged to carry out a
number of chores for his father-in-law during
the first two years of the marriage. Even at the
end of the twentieth century, this unique kinship
system is still flourishing, creating a strong sense
of both ethnic and family identity for Kachins,
wherever they live or travel.

SHAN STATE

Shan State covers a vast highland plateau the size
of England and Wales in north-east Burma. Shan
nationalist groups claim that ethnic Shans make
up just over half of the state's estimated 6 million
people. Other significant ethnic groups with
100,000 or more inhabitants in Shan State include
the Palaung, Wa, Kachin, Danu, Lahu, Akha and
Pa-O. Each has its own distinctive culture and
language.

After the sack of Pagan in 1287 AD by the
Mongols, the Shans nearly succeeded in creating
their own empire, but internal rivalries ultimately
prevented them, although for many centuries they
did rival the powers of the Burman and Mon
kings. By 1500, more than 30 sub-states had
evolved in the region which were ruled by royal
sawbwas or princes.

Under the British Frontier Areas Administration,
the 'Federated Shan States' remained under
the rule of the *sawbwa* families, who were
allowed to retain their personal fiefdoms. Only at
independence in 1948 was the region merged into
one state – Shan State – and incorporated into the
new Union of Burma.

The 1947 constitution guaranteed the right of
secession after a ten-year period in recognition of
the historic independence of the Shan territories.
The *sawbwas*, too, were allowed to keep many of
their traditional feudal rights.

**OLD MARU TAKING COVER
BEHIND SHIELD**
According to legend, all the Kachin
peoples, including the Maru, stem
from a group of six brothers.

James Henry Green Collection, 1920s

MARU DOG TRADERS
In Burma, a number of hill peoples,
including the Maru, traditionally
considered dog flesh a delicacy.

James Henry Green Collection, 1920s

Shortly after independence, an uprising broke out among Pa-O hill-farmers in the south-west who objected to *sawbwa* rule. Relations then deteriorated further in the early 1950s when several thousand exiled Kuomintang invaded Shan State from China in a CIA-backed campaign, and the government sent in the Burmese armed forces to try and quell all opposition. It was the Kuomintang who encouraged the local opium trade, setting up international export markets, and also showed young Shan nationalists the potential for armed resistance.

In 1958–9, General Ne Win persuaded the *sawbwas* to sign an agreement renouncing all their hereditary rights, although this merely encouraged young Shan nationalists to join the underground resistance movement. Within a few years of Ne Win's military coup in March 1962,

uprisings had spread across Shan State to virtually every ethnic group. A major insurrection also broke out in the east of the state through the Chinese-backed Communist Party of Burma, which in 1968 launched an invasion from China.

Throughout the 1970s and 1980s, Shan, Palaung, Kachin, Pa-O, Lahu, Kayan and Wa ethnic forces established their own 'liberated zones' in the mountains, and, under pressure from the Communist Party of Burma (CPB), split into pro- or anti-communist factions. The consequences of these wars for the peoples of Shan State have been tragic. Tens of thousands of soldiers and villagers from every ethnic background have died. According to Anti-Slavery International, once prosperous valleys have been cleared of all habitation by the Burmese armed forces as entire communities have been driven deeper into the mountains where, for many, opium has become the only cash crop.

In 1989, the CPB collapsed to be replaced by five breakaway ethnic minority forces, led by the Wa. Ceasefires were agreed with the State Law and Order Restoration Council (SLORC) government, which subsequently made truces with other ethnic opposition forces, including the Mong Tai Army of the opium kingpin, Khun Sa. However, with

MARU GIRL
Large earrings are one of the most
distinctive features of traditional Maru
and Kachin costume.

James Henry Green Collection,1920s

TWO LASHI WOMEN
The Lashi are closely related
to the Maru, with whom many
have intermarried.

James Henry Green Collection, 1920s

LASHI YOUTH
Today, most Lashi can still be found
living in the area of the N'Mai Hka
River valley.

James Henry Green Collection, 1920s

no lasting agreements, the political outlook for Shan State remains very uncertain.

Culture and language across the State continue to be dominated by the majority Shans, who – along with the Karens – constitute the second largest ethnic group in Burma after the Burmans. An ethnic Tai people, the Shans are closely related to the Siamese of Thailand and Lao people in Laos, who migrated into South-east Asia from Yunnan province, south-west China, around the same time. Many Shans also inhabit Kachin State and northern Burma, and they have also spread through the Hukawng valley into Assam.

Living mainly in the valleys, the **Shan** are traditionally traders and wet-rice cultivators, although they are also very artistic and are well known for their lacquerware and crafts. Traditionally, land within a Shan sub-state belonged to a *sawbwa*, and if a village was founded within the state, its lands were

controlled by the village headman appointed by the *sawbwa*. Farmers and their descendants had rights to the land as long as they paid rent and taxes to the *sawbwa*. If the farmer moved outside the state, he lost his rights. Most of the *sawbwas* were ethnic Shans, but this system was widely emulated and, across the centuries, ethnic Pa-Os, Palaungs and Was also rose to similar rank.

Great social changes have occurred during the political volatility of the past fifty years. Traditional Shan society was divided into nobility and commoners, with a low-caste group which consisted of fishermen, butchers and other occupations which Buddhists generally consider 'unclean'. Most of the population became classed as commoners, although marriage into nobility did occur since feudal relations and territories were constantly being redefined.

Wedding ceremonies, which are witnessed by friends and relatives at the bride's home, still often

involve a village elder tying a white thread around the wrists of the couple, who are then led back to the groom's parents' home.

The Shans have embraced Theravadha Buddhism, particularly in the north, west and south of the state, although they retain a number of occult practices, including charms and spells for curing illnesses, astrology, and divination by dreams.

Tattooing is also an important ritual for Shan boys, as it is regarded as a sign of manhood. The designs on a man's legs, chest, back or arms include occult charms which are supposed to protect him against evil. Such practices have remained popular among soldiers in the fighting of the past few decades.

A few communities exist in the Shan State of the *Yao* (or Man or Mien) people, who are thought by some historians to be the original inhabitants of south China. The Yaos were driven from Hunan province in the twelfth and thirteenth centuries and dispersed widely across South-east Asia, including into Thailand, Vietnam and Laos, from where they are believed to have entered Burma. In the 1950s, it was estimated that there were around 800,000 Yao speakers in South-east Asia, including 660,000 in mainland China. They are related to Hmongs (see below), who share a similar language which, like Yao, has been tentatively identified as Sino-Tibetan in type.

Although their diaspora has meant that Yaos have had to adapt to different types of agriculture, most practise slash-and-burn farming at relatively high altitudes, but below the Hmongs and Lisus. This has historically meant that the Yaos have had more contact with missionaries and traders who lived in the plains.

The Yaos keep domestic animals, particularly pigs, which they trade for salt and metals. They are renowned blacksmiths and silversmiths and also make excellent paper, a skill they probably learned from the Chinese and Tais. Although they brew alcohol and grow opium poppies, they are not heavy drinkers and, unlike some ethnic groups, few are opium addicts. Their preferred stimulants are tea and tobacco.

LISU HOUSE AT AGETU
The Lisu live at some of the
highest altitudes of all the hill
peoples in South-east Asia

James Henry Green Collection, 1920s

of chants written in corrupt Chinese
characters. The sons of wealthy Yao
families are instructed in the priests'
chanting rituals so that they may
become *mo kung* when they grow up.

There is very little information about
the early history and migrations of
the *Hmong*, a related and more
numerous Sino-Tibetan people also
known as the Miao or Meo. Their
name is thought by some scholars to
be derived from the Vietnamese term
'Man Meo', 'Man' being the term
used by early Chinese historians to
refer to all non-Han peoples (except
Tai) in southern China. The Hmongs,
like the Yaos, are probably among
the earliest inhabitants of China. The
Chinese recognised them as an
ethnically distinct group in the
pre-Han dynasty period, when they
appeared in the lower Yangtze River
area and later the Yellow River.

Under pressure from the Chinese,
however, Hmong migrants have
fanned out over the centuries into
Yunnan province in China, Vietnam,
Laos, Thailand and the periphery of
Burma's eastern borderlands. Hmong
culture shows many historical aspects
of other cultures, including Chinese, Lolo, Tai and
Yao, gathered along the way, and they are among
the most prosperous of the hill peoples in South-
east Asia. A long history of migration has made
them adaptable, while a working knowledge of
Chinese has made them successful traders.

LISU GRAVES
Traditional Lisu culture displays
many characteristics of China,
where the Lisu originated.

James Henry Green Collection, 1920s

In South-east Asia, a few have converted to
Christianity, but traditional societies still practise
ancestor-worship and hold their priest-exorcists –
or *mo kung* – in high regard. As well as officiating
at important festivals, such as the harvest time,
the *mo kung* exorcises evil spirits during illness
and divines chicken bones and bamboo sticks for
villagers with problems. They also possess books

The Hmong today are divided into different sub-
groups and clans, according to peculiarities of
dress and speech, such as the Blue Hmong, whose
women weave the hemp skirts which they later
dye indigo, and the White Hmong, who wear
long decorated aprons over their trousers. Along
with the Lisus, the Hmongs are among the most
important opium cultivators in the region. In
the past, opium made many rich and even today
some Hmong men take more than one wife if

they can afford the bride price and are able to support more than one family financially.

Shamans, who may be male or female, are common in most Hmong villages. Their practices are believed to be ancient, showing both Central Asian origins and association with the Taoist mystics of China. In some areas, superstition dictates that a newborn child is part of the spirit world until the baby is three days' old, when chickens are sacrificed and the spirit is called to reside in the baby's body, and the child is named.

Hmong courtship ritual is also interesting. It takes place in January and involves a game in which boys and girls aged around sixteen stand opposite each other in two rows. Each then throws a cotton ball to the girl or boy of their choice. If the ball is caught, then a match can be made. Whoever fails to catch the ball must give presents of silver or clothing to their partner, which also provides the opportunity for further meetings.

Another minority group of people in Shan State are the Chinese. Chinese groups, of different ethnic origins, have entered the territory over the centuries. The Kokang sub-state in the far north is almost entirely Chinese.

One distinctive group are the *Panthay*, as they were known in British days, or Hui-Hui as they call themselves. Often living on the fringes of other communities, the Panthays are Chinese Muslims who originally came to Burma as muleteers on the trade routes between China and Burma.

They are thought to have mixed origins, most likely as descendants of Persian, Arab and Central Asian Muslim traders who migrated to China in the thirteenth and fourteenth centuries and became naturalised. The Panthay became famous as caravan drivers, taking goods from China as far south as Rangoon and Moulmein. Their main occupation was trade and they reputedly used slaves to carry out their domestic work.

The *Lisu* are a Tibeto-Burman people who speak a language which is is closely related to both Lahu and Akha, although many Lisu men may also speak Yunnanese, Shan or Jinghpaw. Anthropologists believe that the Lisus originated in the area north-west of Yunnan in China, and many Lisus continue to identify very closely with the Chinese. Over the centuries, Lisus spread southwards into Thailand as well as Burma,

TWO PALAUNGS
The Palaung, or Ta-ang, are a
Buddhist people who live in the
mountains of Shan State.

James Henry Green Collection, 1920s

where they live in scattered communities, predominantly in the upper Salween region of Shan State and in the Kachin Hills.

Their contiguity with Kachins in Kachin State has meant that Lisu clans have been identified with Kachin clans and both peoples have intermarried. The Chinese historically referred to the Lisu as the 'Yeh-jen' or 'wild people', which was later corrupted by the Kachins to Yawyin or Yaw-yen. British colonial administrators also knew the Lisus as Yawyins and often referred to them by this name in their accounts of Burma and in records of service in the First World War, where Lisu battalions fought alongside the British.

Lisu villages are usually built on high ridges and mountain tops up to 9,000 feet. They prefer inaccessible spots which can be easily defended, usually hidden away among dense thickets of bamboo. Although they keep animals, the Lisus are mainly farmers, cultivating rice, buckwheat, vegetables and, very often, opium. However, although they have produced a great deal of the opium in the Golden Triangle region, few are addicted to the drug, although they do use it for medicine.

Lisus can frequently be seen in the rotating markets of Shan State, where they sell bamboo work, baskets and weaving as well as opium, firewood and herbs. They have traditionally acted as middlemen between Yunnanese traders and the other hill peoples in Burma.

The Lisu believe that they are the only people to have survived the great flood, and some claim that all their clans in the mountains of South-east Asia originate from a brother and sister who survived the deluge. Hereditary chiefs normally control several Lisu villages in an area and they impose the law and judge crimes.

In Shan State, the Lisus appear to have been little touched by either Christian or Buddhist influences. Their religion does, however, contain elements of Taoism and involves ancestor worship and propitiation of spirits of the jungle, wind, earth, sky, village and crops. Each village has a spirit doctor who treats illnesses which are thought to involve malevolent spirits, and acts as an intermediary to the spirit world, warding off harm with chants, sacrifices and charms.

The annual spring festival is the high point of the year, when villagers celebrate for up to six days, honouring their ancestors and visiting the graves of relatives who have recently died. It is also the time when young boys and girls can meet each other and marriage matches can be made.

The *Palaung*, who live mainly in the north-western corner of Shan State, are descended from Mon-Khmer stock and are thought to be among the earliest inhabitants of Burma, preceding the Burmans, Shans and Kachins. The name Palaung is Burmese; the Palaungs call themselves Ta-ang. They can also be found in the southern part of Kachin State and in Yunnan province.

Their homeland consists of high ridges of up to 6,000 feet separated by narrow valleys. Palaung villages are usually small and built on hill-tops or ridges between hills. They are famous for their

traditional long-houses and for growing tea on the steep slopes; mules are used to negotiate the difficult terrain during the harvesting season when entire villages are employed in picking and processing the tea. The Palaungs also cultivate rice, beans, hemp, yams, chillies and sugar-cane among other crops. Men and women smoke tobacco and chew betel nuts, but tea is generally considered a man's drink.

Palaungs trade their tea (both pickled and dried) and livestock for silver jewellery, cloth, kerosene, salt, betel nuts, preserved fish and milk. Trade is carried out at markets in Palaung villages or the towns of Shan State – and also outside their homeland as far away as Mandalay and Rangoon. They do not trade their own crafts, which include cloth and baskets.

Until the early years after independence, Palaung society was structured in a similar way to the Shans under the feudal princes or *sawbwas*, most of whom were ethnic Shans, who controlled the different valley-states. In the Tawngpeng sub-state, however, the ruler was a Palaung.

Armed conflict, which broke out following General Ne Win's 1962 coup, inflicted considerable destruction and loss of life until a 1991 ceasefire. But many villages are still ruled by

PALAUNGS IN LAWSAWK STATE 1905
Palaungs are known as Gold or Silver according to their dress.

British Library/Oriental and India Office Collection

headmen, who traditionally answer to clan chiefs who control groups of villages. Headmen deal with minor law cases, while chiefs look at more serious cases. Wealth defines status in the village, and servants who receive wages for picking tea are regarded as inferior to families who own land. There are records, too, of witches, whose power is thought to be passed down from their mothers, living in a separate part of the village.

Courting tends to take place during harvesting in the tea gardens or at the girl's house, where boys must woo her through holes in the floor of her bedroom. Young people often congregate at the village monastery, which is also a school for boys. Palaungs are Buddhists and, according to legend, Theravada Buddhism was introduced to them at the insistence of Burman kings around 1780, although it probably came much earlier through contact with the Shans.

Most of the Palaung ceremonies are Buddhist ones, but they also hold an annual spirit festival in September. They believe in two kinds of spirits: *kar-bu*, spirits of animals and men which survive death for around a week, and *kar-nam*, which are the spirits of plants and inanimate objects. Each person has two guardian spirits and there are spirits of the house, village, roads, tea crops and so on.

After the Shans, the *Pa-O* are the largest ethnic group in the Shan State. They are a branch of the Karen peoples and live mainly around Taunggyi in south-west Shan State. The Burmans usually refer to the Pa-O as Taungthu, which means 'hill people' in Burmese. The exact origins of the Pa-O remains uncertain, because a large group of Pa-Os – about 70,000 in total – also live much further to the south in the Thaton area of Lower Burma. To account for this, Pa-Os have a tradition that their migration north began 900 years ago with the overthrow of the Mon kingdom at Thaton by Anawrahta of Pagan in 1057. Certainly, like the Mons of Lower Burma, the Pa-Os have a long tradition of Buddhism.

Pa-O terrain in Shan State, which is centred on the old sub-state of Hsa-Htung, is a mixture of mountain, open forest and lowland, where they cultivate rice, vegetables and fruit. Their main cash crop is the leaves from the cordia trees which are used for rolling Burmese cheroots. Hunting is both for food and recreation and Pa-O villagers use spears, crossbow, traps and nets. Busy traders, Pa-O communities were once regarded as prosperous, but, like the Shans and local hill

peoples, many Pa-O villages have been badly affected by the political violence that broke out in their region in 1949. Pa-O leaders still dream of the creation of a Pa-O special region or state, and local ceasefires with the SLORC government by Pa-O armed forces in the early 1990s mean that this demand has been discussed in Rangoon.

Pa-O villages are often noted for the beauty of the magnificent wooden monasteries which they build, and Buddhist practices dominate community life. However, along with other Buddhist or ethnic groups in Burma, they also worship *Nats* or spirits, such as tree or house *Nats*, and *Nat* shrines can usually be found outside villages or near pagodas, where offerings can be made.

The nearby hill region above Inle Lake is also the home of the *Taungyo*, who are farmers of Tibeto-Burman descent. Although very little has been recorded of their history, they are thought,

TAUNGTHU BOY DECORATING THE EAR OF A GIRL
The Taungthu, or Pa-O, live in both Karen and Shan States.

James Henry Green Collection, 1920s

TAUNGTHU GIRLS SELLING THATCHING
In Shan State, the main crop of Pa-O
farmers is the *thanapet* leaf, which is used
to roll cheroots.

James Henry Green Collection, 1920s

like the Pa-Os, to have fled many centuries ago
from Lower Burma into the mountain sanctuaries
of this area or to have been brought as prisoners
to Shan State, where they married local women.
Taungyos speak a language which linguists
believe resembles a Rakhine dialect of Burmese,
although the Taungyos themselves dispute this.
Numerically few, they have largely adopted Shan
and Pa-O styles of dress, but Taungyo women
can still be distinguished by heavy rings worn
below the knee.

Little has been written about the **Riang** since the
time of Sir J. G. Scott, the great British explorer
and administrator. Living in a few isolated
mountain areas across Shan State, many Riangs
speak Shan as well as their own language. The
Shans call the three main Riang clans the Yang
Lam, Yang Sek and Yang Wankun, and the Riang
themselves have begun to refer to themselves by
these names. The Burmans call them Yin, hence
the name of two sub-groups, the Yinnet (Black
Riang) and Yinset (Striped Riang), who are
divided according to their different styles of dress.

All three Riang clans believe that they have
occupied their homeland in Shan State since time
immemorial, although some scholars believe they

are relations of the Palaungs and Was
who have migrated to their present
territory, while the Burmese term Yin
is more commonly used to describe
Karens.

Many Riangs are rapidly adopting
Shan dress and customs. However,
both the Yang Wankun and Yang Sek
have retained their traditional
courtship dances, which they perform
enthusiastically at festivals. Unlike
some ethnic groups, both men and
women take part in the dances,
which involve singing to the music
of traditional reed pipes.

South-east of the Riangs, around
Kengtung, live the *Akha*, a Tibeto-
Burman people related to the Lahu
and Lisu who originated in Yunnan province in
south China and have been migrating south for
centuries. Akhas are also found in Yunnan, Laos
and northern Thailand, where their cultures have
been more closely studied. They are said to be
divided into between seven and nine major clans,
which represent a large group of brothers from
whom all Akhas are supposed to have descended.

Akhas live above the plains in the mountains,
but below the villages of the Hmongs, Lisus and
Lahus, in houses built on stilts which jut out of
the mountainside. Because Akhas are afraid of
water spirits, their villages are built at some
distance from water, and a conduit of bamboo
pipes is used to bring water from the source.
They practise slash-and-burn agriculture and
traditionally move their villages every five to ten
years, or when the soil becomes depleted.

According to Akha myth, humans and spirits once
lived in harmony on earth, with humans tilling the
fields during the day and the spirits doing so at
night. Trouble broke out when the spirits began
to steal eggs from humans and humans began to
steal cucumbers from the spirits. Therefore Akhas
built spirit gates at the entrances to all their
villages, to separate the realm of the spirits from
that of humans.

Beside the gates are male and female fertility
figures carved in wood, which act as a warning to
jungle spirits that they are approaching the
dwellings of humans and must stay away. Draped
around the pillars of the spirit gates are rings of
bamboo which link together, holding crossed
bamboo slats to keep malevolent spirits at bay.

KAW VILLAGE
High in the mountains, the
houses of the Kaw or Akha people
are raised on stilts.

James Henry Green Collection, 1920s

It is important that visitors do not touch any part of the spirit gate of an Akha village as a cleansing ceremony for the community would then be necessary. Akhas feel extremely vulnerable when they enter the forest because it is the domain of the spirits; when they return to the village, they pass through the gates to cleanse themselves of spirits they may have encountered in the forest.

As well as practising agriculture, the Akhas rear domestic animals, including cattle, buffalo and horses, which they sell for cash. Opium is an important cash crop, which the Akhas exchange for goods that they cannot obtain in the hills. Much of their silver has been bought from valley-dwellers such as the Shans and Chinese.

In recent years, Akha communities have become increasingly poor. There are many opium addicts among the Akha people and when they run up debts, they sometimes sell or give away their children for payment. Since the late 1980s, many young Akha women have also migrated into prostitution in neighbouring Thailand, where high rates of HIV-infection have been recorded among sex workers.

The Akhas of Burma celebrate the usual harvest and New Year festivals, but they also hold an unusual ceremony in which villagers take turns on a huge village swing during a three-day festival. This is accompanied by animal sacrifices and other rituals designed to rid the village of any evil spirits.

As well as meeting at these festivals, young Akha boys and girls can meet freely at village courting grounds. Sexual relations take place at an early age among the Akhas and are accepted – often a couple will disappear into the forest for the night. A girl or boy may have as many sexual adventures as they wish and a girl becomes more desirable once she has given birth. When a couple decides to marry, a bride price is paid and the couple celebrate a wedding where the friends smear their

KAW MAN AND PIPE
Music plays an important role in
traditional Akha ceremonies.

James Henry Green Collection, 1920s

KAW WOMAN WEAVING
Like other hill peoples, Akhas
have learnt to be self-sufficient and
produce their own cloth.

James Henry Green Collection, 1920s

The *Lahu* are another Tibeto-Burman ethnic family who probably originated in Tibet or close to the Tibetan border. Along with Akhas and Lisus, they are believed to have descended from the ancient Lolo people. There are perhaps as many as 150,000 Lahus in Burma, who live close to the Akhas near Kengtung in south-east Shan State. In recent years, Lahus from Burma have also spread to Laos and Thailand, where they inhabit rugged hill country, usually around 4,000 feet or above.

Some Lahus have a tradition that their ancestors came from near the Irrawaddy River, although their appearance and customs suggest they are Tibetan in origin. The Chinese called them Lohei or by the Tai name Muser, which means 'hunter', referring to their formidable reputation as hunters and warriors. They have a long history of warfare against the encroachment of others, including the Chinese in south-west Yunnan. Even today, Lahu men compete for the title of 'supreme hunter' which gives them an exalted position in the community.

The Lahus are divided into various clans, such as the Lahu Na (Black, Great or Independent Lahu), who mostly live in Burma and Yunnan; the Lahu Nyi (Southern or Red Lahu), an offshoot of the Lahu Na in Burma and Thailand; and the Lahu

faces with ash from the bottom of the cooking pot and traditionally throw mud and dung at them to initiate them into married life.

When an Akha dies, a large tree is felled and hollowed out into a coffin in the shape of a boat with wings at the ends. Another log is hewn for the lid which must fit perfectly. When the coffin is completed, it is put outside the house of the deceased and everyone in the village pours liquor over it. The body is then put into the coffin and covered in a black shroud and a red cloth and the genealogy of the dead person is recited for the first time, along with their name. After a few days, the coffin is buried.

In normal conversation, the Akha never use their real names because they believe names have a magical significance – if the spirits hear their names, they will have power over the Akhas.

KAW GIRLS DANCING TO MAN AND PIPE
The women of the various Akha
clans can be distinguished by their ornate
head-dresses.

James Henry Green Collection, 1920s

Shi (Yellow Lahu) also in Burma, Yunnan and Thailand. The various clans differ in dialect and details of dress, but they retain common basic religious observances and settlement patterns.

Lahus rely on slash-and-burn agriculture, cultivating rice, vegetables and chilli. In Burma, they have been closely involved in the cultivation of opium, which they use themselves and trade for salt and metal. Although they have trading links with the Lisu, Akha and Wa, most mountain Lahus rarely speak Burmese, Shan or other languages. By contrast, a number of other ethnic groups often use Lahu as the lingua franca for trade in the southern hill regions.

Village chiefs traditionally control Lahu affairs, often assisted by the priest-shaman – or *pawku* – who is an important figure in Lahu society. In some villages, the *pawku* is elevated to village leader with influence over a wide area. One example of a powerful *pawku* was a priest in the Kengtung area who claimed he had a magic knife, rope and hammer with which he could destroy enemies, even prompting some Lahus in Thailand to return to Burma.

Individual warriors – called *po* – can be appointed to impose penalties or fines for wrong-doing, although serious cases are decided by divination,

with penalties ranging from losing a hand to death. In more remote areas, villagers accused of possessing an evil spirit may be banished from the village.

Although maintaining many traditional practices, entire villages have been known to convert to Christianity under the village chief's orders. At the turn of the century, the American evangelist William H. Young opened the first Baptist mission in Kengtung to preach to Lahus.

Earlier, a Lahu prophet had told his followers that a sign would appear in the form of a white man riding a white horse and bearing the scriptures of god. When Reverend Young rode into the Shan states carrying a Bible, some Lahus reputedly decided he was their god and thousands of them came to be baptised. In 1932 he retired, but his son, Harold Young, converted many thousands more Lahus and in 1935 he opened a new mission in the Wa sub-state. By 1950, an estimated 28,000 of the 66,000 Lahus in north-eastern Burma had been converted to Christianity.

In the view of some historians, these combined shaman and Christian influences furthered the rise of the local Guisha cult, where followers believe in the powers of 'man-god' prophets. Indeed, it was one such elderly chieftain and prophet who initiated a Lahu uprising against the Burmese government in 1972. Dozens of Lahu villages were subsequently relocated or destroyed in fighting, which continued in the mountains of the Mong Hsat area until the 1990s.

The *Intha* people live around Lake Inle in south-west Shan State near Taunggyi. Like the Taungyos, they are Tibeto-Burman, but they speak a dialect closer to Burmese. As a result, they are thought by some historians to be the descendants of slaves taken captive by Burman kings in the wars with the Mons and Tavoyans, or southern Burmans who migrated north during the reign of King Narapatisithu (1174–1210). The majority are Buddhists, and today most of them wear Burmese dress – a longyi and an open-necked shirt or blouse.

Having arrived in Shan State, the Inthas seem to have been moved from the best land and on to the lake by more powerful ethnic groups already in the region. It was there that they developed their unique ability for farming and catching fish. The Inthas are often called 'children of the lake' as they build houses on stilts over the shallow waters and weave beds of water hyacinths together into

AKHA KAW, SHAN STATES, 1905
Akha men and women in full
ceremonial dress.

*British Library/ Oriental and India
Office Collection*

NAWNLENG YANGSEK GIRLS, c. 1905
The Yangsek are a sub-group of
the Riang people in Shan State.

*British Library/Oriental and India
Office Collection*

according to their legends, they
have inhabited the area since the
beginning of time.

The name Wa is thought to have
Shan origins and has been widely
accepted by the Wa themselves. The
Shans and British also distinguished
between what they termed 'wild' or
uncivilised Wa and the 'tame' Wa
who had converted to Buddhism.
There are also a great number of
peoples in the Shan State who speak
a Wa-related language, including the
Riang and Palaung, and over the
centuries many traditional Was are
believed to have assimilated Shan or
other ethnic identities. In a number
of valleys, Wa chieftains also
imitated the Shan *sawbwa* system.

long floating baskets of up to 30 feet, filling them
with rich earth in which they cultivate vegetables
and flowers. These soil beds are not anchored and
can be navigated like a canoe by paddling to any
area on the lake.

As well as weaving, for which they are famous
throughout Burma, the Inthas are best known for
their unique one-legged rowing technique.
Standing on their long, narrow boats, they wrap
one leg round the paddle, holding it with one
hand, and propel the boat forward, balancing
on the other leg. They then use their free arm to
push conical bamboo fish traps under the water
to catch fish.

WA SUB-STATE

The *Wa* are a people of Mon-Khmer ancestry,
who live in a semi-autonomous region in the
eastern part of Shan State bordering China. By
some estimates, there are around 300,000 Was
in Burma, and perhaps as many as 2 million
Was and closely related Palaungs in the great
mountain wilderness where the borders of Burma,
China and Thailand meet. The Was may well
be the oldest inhabitants of this region, and,

True 'wild' Wa country was a mountainous region
spreading over 150 miles north–south along the
Chinese border between the Salween and Mekong
Rivers. This region was virtually impenetrable to
both the British and Chinese in colonial days. But
many Wa communities can also be found outside
this territory, especially around Kengtung. A few
villages of the related Lawa have also survived in
the Thai border area.

Wa country consists of high mountain ranges,
which plunge into valleys 2,000 to 5,000 feet
deep. Wa peoples build villages on the higher
mountain slopes, away from streams, which are
thought to cause fever; water is often piped into
the village in a bamboo aqueduct. Villages can
have as many as three hundred houses and were
traditionally protected by a six-feet high earth
rampart covered with thorn bushes and thickets.
A deep concealed ditch is often dug around the
perimeter of the village for extra protection, and
entrance to the village is by means of a long
narrow tunnel which is closed near the village
by a heavy wooden door.

Extensive cultivation has left many of the hills in
the region deforested, and Wa villagers often have
to rely on hunting and fishing for food. They also
rear animals and grow some crops, including
opium, which has become their main cash crop.
They exchange opium for foodstuffs and metal,
which they know how to work. Some Was also
make their own guns, gunpowder and lead bullets.

Because of their proximity to the Chinese border,
between 1968 and 1989 the Was came under the

influence of the Communist Party of Burma, which launched an invasion of the Shan State from China. For two decades, fierce fighting continued in the mountains and over 20,000 Was are reported to have died. In 1989, however, a local Wa rebellion overthrew the CPB leadership and a newly-formed United Wa State Party assumed control of the area before agreeing a ceasefire with the SLORC government in Rangoon.

Most of the Wa mountains, nevertheless, remain off-limits to travellers, largely because of the opium trade. There are scattered Shan and Chinese settlements in their region, the latter

MIXED GROUP LAHUS
Three major clans of the Lahu people inhabit the Chinese, Thai, Lao and Burmese borderlands. Tibeto-Burmans, they are related to the Akha and Lisu, who inhabit many of the same mountains.

James Henry Green Collection, 1920s

being used as middlemen in the opium trade. But Wa villagers do not have much contact with other ethnic groups, except for the Lahus who mostly live further to the south where Wa forces have recently advanced.

Historically, too, Was have been isolated, not least because of their formidable reputation for head-hunting, which they practised until recently as part of their fertility rites. Only twenty years ago, the headless corpses of their victims could still be found outside a few Wa settlements.

Indeed, on the way to Kengtung one village was said to have had 300 human skulls on display beside the road.

In the past, most Was would rarely leave their villages, except for organised head-hunting trips. These would be carried out by small ambush parties who would travel great distances to find a stray victim. Newly taken heads were put in wicker-work baskets tied to long poles in the village, where they would be left until the flesh rotted and fell away. Some villages had as many as twenty heads decaying in this fashion. Later, they would be ceremoniously positioned in rows in a sacred grove outside the village where they would be placed in the niches of posts.

The custom of head-hunting is thought to relate to Wa mythology, which associates the practice with the legendary founders of the Wa race. They are regarded as protection against evil spirits; without skulls, the Was believed that their families would die and their crops fail, which would be a calamity for them and also enrage their ancestors.

The heads of strangers were always favoured because it was thought that the spirit or ghost which would linger around the skull would not know his way out of the hills and thus stay close to his remains. New heads were particularly important during the spring planting season.

KAYAH STATE

More than a dozen ethnic groups live in modern-day Kayah State, formerly Karenni State, a rugged mountain region in eastern Burma nestling between Shan State to the north, Karen State to the west and south, and Thailand to the east. They include the Padaung, Bre, Yinbaw, Paku and Kayah, who form the largest ethnic group. There is also a Shan minority in several valley areas.

The culture of the local people, generally known as *Karenni* or Red Karens, is predominantly Karen. Although Karenni leaders claim ancient traditions of independence, some scholars believe that the idea of a separate Karenni identity stems from the more recent custom of local chieftains copying the Shan system of ruling princes, or *sawbwas*. These hereditary titles were acknowledged by the Burman King Mindon and formally recognised in 1875 by a treaty of the British during the annexation of the country. As a result, the Karenni State was never fully incorporated into British Burma.

SHAN STATE, *c.* 1905
A rare early photograph of the 'Wild Wa', who
lived in the eastern mountains of Shan State.

*British Library/Oriental and India
Office Collection*

Under the 1947 constitution, Karenni
State – like the Shan State – was
granted the right of secession after a
ten-year period within the Union of
Burma, but in August 1948, the
Karenni leader U Bee Htu Re was
assassinated by central government
militia, and an armed uprising swept
the state that has continued to the
present day.

With this backdrop of conflict, successive
governments have failed to satisfy Karenni
grievances. The state was renamed Kayah State
in 1951, with the intention, some historians claim,
of making a divisive distinction between the
Karennis and their close Karen relatives, both of
whom have been fighting for greater autonomy.
The legal right of secession was finally written
out of the 1974 constitution.

As elsewhere in Burma, many local ethnic groups
have suffered in the conflict of the past five
decades. Entire communities have been forced to
relocate, and government anti-insurgency
operations have displaced large numbers of hill
peoples. Increasing numbers of government
troops have been deployed across the state to
control and open up vast forest tracks to Thai
loggers who, in the 1990s, stripped many of the
mountainsides bare. During 1994–5, ceasefires
were agreed between the SLORC government and
the three main ethnic opposition forces, but the
peace has yet to stabilise, and villagers have
continued to flee into Thailand, where around
12,000 Karennis are living in refugee camps.

The largest ethnic group in Kayah State are the
Kayah. There are estimated to be more than
150,000 living in Burma, mostly in Kayah State.
Along with the Sgaw, Pwo and Pa-O, the Kayah
are one of the main linguistic and cultural groups
among the Karen people, who live in much of
Lower Burma and the Thai borderlands. It is
from their distinctively coloured head cloths or
shawls that the Karenni peoples have gained the
name 'Red Karen'.

Like other hill-dwelling Karens, Kayah villagers
practise slash-and-burn agriculture and hunt and

WA MAN
The Wa hills have been badly
denuded in the past century. Opium
today is the major cash crop.

James Henry Green Collection, 1920s

217

fish to supplement their diets. They trade cotton cloth and forest products for food, pottery, metal and other materials. Trade is sometimes conducted with itinerant merchants, but Kayahs can often be seen in local markets, and in the past century many Kayahs have moved to the towns.

In the past, most Kayahs were traditional spirit worshippers, but significant numbers have converted to Christianity, especially Baptists or Catholics. The most important festival of the year is the Kathowbow Festival, which is held sometime between March and May, during which Kayahs and other Karennis – including Christians, Buddhists and animists today – pay homage to the rain spirits.

Little has been recorded by historians of the history of the **Bre** (or Kayaw), but they are close relatives of the Kayah. Until recently, many preferred to live in remote forests, a behaviour some anthropologists believe stems from a time when larger and more powerful ethnic groups in the region preyed on them or captured them in slave raids. Like their neighbours, the Padaung, Bre society is matriarchal and lineage is reckoned through women.

One documented custom of the Bre is the ritual bathing of babies every morning and evening for a year after their birth. In traditional villages, Bres consider this to be enough cleansing for a lifetime and do not encourage the child to wash after their first year. The right to name the child rests with the mother, who, after consulting chicken bones with the village shaman, will decide if the child is to be named after its grandfather (for a boy) or grandmother (for a girl).

The **Padaung** live in a few mountain locations in the Kayah and Shan State borderlands. They call themselves Ka-Kaung and speak a Karenic language, which is considered a sub-group of Kayan. Despite their relatively small population (estimated at up to 50,000), they are probably the most well-known of all Burma's hill peoples because of the distinctive brass coils which the women wear around their necks. These rings, which can weigh anything up to twenty-five pounds, push the collar bone and shoulders down, elongating the neck, which has given rise to the nickname 'giraffe women', or 'long-necked Karens'.

The first ring is usually fitted when the girl is under the age of ten. A village medicine man will decide which is the most auspicious day for the

PADAUNG GIRL PROFILE
A traditional Padaung woman with a full set of brass neck coils.

James Henry Green Collection, 1920s

ceremony. When the day dawns, her neck is massaged for several hours and rubbed with an ointment said to be made of dog fat, coconut milk and royal jelly and the first ring, which is about four inches high, is fitted. A new ring would be added every year until the girl reached a marriageable age. Traditionally, both the legs and arms were also encased with the coils, although few Padaungs have a full set of rings. Padaung women certainly believe that the rings make them look more beautiful, while the arm rings are useful for defending themselves.

The origins of this tradition are unclear, although some scholars believe it was a deliberate action by Padaung men to prevent marauding bandits or other ethnic groups from kidnapping their women. It is unclear whether the rings were designed to make the women look unattractive or to enable the men to chain them to trees or houses (each set of coils has a loop at the back which looks like a chaining ring). Other explanations may be that the Padaungs were keen to protect their women from attacks by tigers or other wild animals in the forest. Some anthropologists also believe that the custom relates to the myth surrounding the origin of the Padaung people. It is said that they were created after a dragon was impregnated by the wind and that the lengthening of the women's necks is supposed to imitate their dragon mother's own long neck.

The Padaungs are skilful agriculturists and every part of the valleys where they live is terraced for irrigation. The women carry out a wide range of chores, despite the heavy weight of their rings. They carry water for household use, hoe the fields, spin cloth and walk long distances to village markets to sell their liquor and other produce. The rings do not seem to affect their health or mobility, although they do walk rather awkwardly and often speak with an unusually high-pitched voice.

The Padaungs were traditionally animists, who, like most other inhabitants of Burma, worshipped a vast array of spirits. In keeping with this practice, they were careful to propitiate malevolent spirits with sacrifices, while friendly spirits would be called upon during festivals and times of celebration. In recent years, a majority of Padaungs have become Catholics, and in many communities a number of traditional

practices – including the wearing of neck-rings – have rapidly declined.

The Padaung region, too, has been badly affected by fighting, and armed nationalist movements, notably the Kayan New Land Party, have frequently operated in or around Padaung villages. As a result, the war and other pressures have sent many as refugees to Thailand, where they make a living posing for photographs for international tourists.

The *Lahta* or Zayein are another Kayan sub-group who live in the rugged pine-forested country west of Pekon and Pinlaung on the Kayah and Shan State borders. They live high up on the mountainside, at around 6,000 feet, where they build villages which are out of reach of their enemies. Like the Padaungs, they cultivate rice on the hillsides and, as the success of their crop depends on rainfall, they must spend hours fetching water from streams.

Every Lahta village has a village elder or spirit master on whom the villagers rely for advice, such as when to marry or when to sow their crops. They are very superstitious: if a woman or an animal gives birth, they will not go into the fields or hunt. They warn the villagers of the birth by hanging a white thread on their stairway. Lahtas also turn away visitors to the village at these times as well as during harvests.

Lahtas have strict rules about courtship: after puberty, a Lahta boy traditionally moves to a communal house called a *haw* with his unmarried male relatives. When the men and boys go to the fields to work, an old man guards the bachelor house and no woman is ever allowed inside. Until they marry, the only time that boys and girls can meet is at funerals or while working in the fields.

If a couple wants to marry, the advice of the spirit master is sought and he consults chicken bones into which bamboo needles are inserted. The right side of the chicken's femur relates to the man and the left to the woman: if the needles stand up

THESE PADAUNG LADIES ARE WELL AWARE OF THEIR IMPORTANCE (1905)
A traditional group photograph.

British Library/Oriental and India Office Collection

straight, it is a good sign; if they match roughly, it should be a reasonable pairing. If they do not match, another time is chosen, when the bones are consulted once again.

The marriage is dependent on the parents, who set up the union when children are small. Until recently, boys and girls had no say in the matter. If the children disagree with their parents' choice, they are allowed to elope, but they are cut off from the Lahta community as other villages will not accept them. There are reputedly entire villages in Kayah State composed of people who ran away from their villages in order to marry.

If a match is agreed upon, either the groom pays the bride price or the bride herself will pay for her husband in silver coins. The price can be anything up to 30 rupees for a boy and 20 for a girl, although sometimes much more is paid. The rupees come from India and some are more than a century old. Lahtas are only allowed to marry during one month of the year, the month being decided by the spirit master. If they do not marry in that month, they must wait another year.

The *Yinbaw* are another sub-group of the Kayan Karens, who live in the Kantarawaddy and Bawlahke regions of Kayah State. They live on the plains rather than on mountain tops, a custom which results in them calling themselves the 'Kang-ngan' or 'plains-dwellers'. In earlier times, like other Karennis, they recognised the authority of four or five *sawbwa* families who politically controlled the state, but at the local level administration is still governed by the headmen and elders.

In common with Kayahs and other Karennis, Yinbaws have strict rules concerning marriage and are usually monogamous. Formerly they were animists, but most have converted to Christianity within the past century. However, once a year the Yinbaw still celebrate the Karenni spirit festival of Kathowbow, when men and women sing together, unlike Lahtas, whose men would sing a refrain, to be answered by the women.

KAREN STATE

Karen State lies south of Kayah State and stretches downwards along the western Thai border to the Tenasserim Division. It is homeland to around a million of Burma's Karens, or around a quarter of the total ethnic Karen population. Since Burma gained independence in 1948, Karen nationalists have been fighting for autonomy and, until the 1990s, the main insurgent force, the Karen National Union (KNU), controlled much of the mountain borderlands adjoining Thailand. Recent Burmese army victories, however, and internal splits have seen the KNU lose most of its permanent base areas.

Despite this long-running conflict, the *Karen* and related sub-groups have been very little documented in Burma. This is the more surprising because they probably constitute, along with the Shans, the second largest ethnic group in the country after the Burmans. They live throughout much of Lower Burma, from the Arakan Yoma and Delta region right up to the Pegu Yoma highlands, the Shan State and Thai borderlands.

Anthropologists and linguists have identified more than twenty sub-groups among the Karens, but, in general, there are just four main divisions: the Sgaw, Pwo and the Kayah or Karenni. More than

YINBAO KAREN, SHAN STATE (1905)
The dress of this Yinbaw couple is very similar to the Kayah.

British Library/Oriental and India Office Collection

**BRE MEN AND WOMEN DANCING
AT LOIKAW (1907)**
The Bre are a sub-group of Karennis.

*British Library/Oriental and
India Office Collection*

The majority of Karens are Pwo and Sgaw wet-rice agriculturalists who often live alongside Burman and, in some areas, Mon villages in the plains and valleys, where they also grow fruit and vegetables. In the hills, hunting is carried out as a pastime as well as a way of gathering food; Karen hunters are sometimes accompanied by specially bred and trained hunting dogs. Hill Karens are also noted for their ability to handle elephants, which they catch and train themselves. Most of Burma's elephant drivers, or *mahouts*, are Karens.

70 per cent of Karens belong to the Sgaw and Pwo sub-groups, and the division of Karen speakers into different regions and sub-cultures is often attributed to the three main routes – along the Irrawaddy, Sittang and Salween Rivers – by which all the Karen peoples are believed to have migrated into Burma.

Ethnic Karens have lived in Burma for more than a thousand years, but practically nothing is known of their early history. Karen mythology refers to a 'river of running sand' which their ancestors are supposed to have crossed. Some scholars have identified this as the sand-drifts of the Gobi Desert in Central Asia, but others feel it could just as easily describe the mighty sand banks along the rivers down which they travelled. The Karen language also has a different word order to Tibeto-Burman languages, with which it has been loosely identified, and influences of Sino-Tibetan as well as long contact with Mons have been noted.

The first reliable historical accounts of the Karens date back to the British annexation of Burma in the nineteenth century, when the Karen language was put into writing. Like the Kachins and Chins, many Karens joined the British army and large numbers converted to Christianity, although the majority remained Buddhist. Many Karens welcomed the British as liberators from historical repression by Burman kings and this, together with the appointment of a number of Karens to senior political and military positions under British rule, led to an ethnic polarisation between the Karen and Burman communities which continues to the present day.

Plains Karen live in similar houses to Burmans and other inhabitants, but in the northern hills there are still a few remote areas where Karens live in traditional long-houses. At one time, an entire community of twenty to thirty families would live in one house, consisting of individual apartments with verandahs opening on to a central corridor. As well as the family quarters, each long-house had a separate room which was used both as a bachelors' room and a guest room.

In the hills, where traditional agricultural practices remain, work is divided fairly equally between men and women, with women fetching water and firewood, preparing rice for cooking, brewing alcoholic drinks and weaving cloth; men hunt, plough, cut timber, build houses and make mats and baskets. Sowing, reaping, threshing and winnowing are done by everyone.

In such areas, animist beliefs are still strong and many villagers believe in supernatural entities, including *Nats,* or nature spirits who control human events, and ghosts of those who died violently or lived evil lives.

Karens traditionally believed that all illness, death and accidents are caused by spirits attacking the vital principle of a person. This vital principle is thought to exist before birth and survives after death, but it can leave the body, causing illness or death. It can also, as a ghost, possess the body of another person.

The events of the past century, however, have had a decisive cultural impact on many Karen societies. About 20 per cent of Sgaw and Pwo Karens have converted to Christianity, many of whom have become leaders of the nationalist movement. Support for Karen nationalism is also strong among the majority Buddhists, but in the Delta region, around such towns as Bassein and Henzada, many Karens have become assimilated into the local Burman community and no longer speak Karen at all.

Only in the eastern mountains has the full diversity of Karen cultures survived. Here the

ZAYEIN KARENS, SHAN STATES (1905)
The Zayein, or Lahta, are one of several Karen-related peoples who live in the deep mountains of the Shan-Karenni borderlands in eastern Burma.

British Library/Oriental and India Office Collection

millennial Telakhon sect still exists in the southern Dawna range. Like the Guisha cult of the Lahus, it combines both Christian and Buddhist teachings and is led by a divine prophet, known as the Phu Chaik or 'Grandfather-Buddha'. Such villagers still repeat the old Karen mythology of a 'Golden Book' stolen by a younger 'White Brother', who one day will return with this book of all knowledge.

The prevalence of this myth is attributed by historians to the early conversions of many Karens to Christianity in the nineteenth century.

Such traditional ways of life are now under serious threat. Community leaders estimate that perhaps a third of all inhabitants of Karen State have been displaced or forcibly relocated by the Burmese army from their homes during the fighting of the past five decades.

More than 100,000 Karen refugees are currently in Thailand, many from some of the remotest villages where no-one is now allowed to live. Even in refugee camps, Karen men can be distinguished by the red tunics that they continue to wear, but leaders fear for the very survival of their culture into the next generation unless there is peace.

MON STATE

Mon State borders the Gulf of Martaban, west of Karen State in Lower Burma. It was created in response to demands for a homeland for Burma's Mons, who took up arms against the Burmese government at the same time as the Karens after independence in 1948. So far, it has done little to quell nationalist dissatisfaction among Mon intellectuals and leaders. Mon culture has been characterised by rapid assimilation into mainstream Burmese culture over the past century. Mon leaders claim a population of 4 million; the government, by contrast, puts the figure at just over a million.

In 1995, a ceasefire was agreed between the SLORC government and the insurgent New Mon State Party, but many villagers have continued to leave their homes inside Burma. According to recent estimates, there are more than 100,000 Mon refugees and illegal migrants in Thailand today, where a few indigenous communities of Mons also still survive.

The *Mon* people are descendants of the Mon-Khmer, one of South-east Asia's most ancient civilisations. It was the Mon inhabitants of Burma who introduced both Buddhism and writing to the country. Well before the Burmans and other Tibeto-Burman peoples had left their homelands in central Asia for their migration south, the Mons had settled into the fertile coastlands along the Gulfs of Siam and Martaban on both sides of the Tenasserim mountain range. They can be considered part of the first wave of migrations into both Burma and old Siam.

**BLACK KAREN WOMAN STANDING
WITH PESTLE AND MORTAR**
Much of the domestic work in Karen
villages is the duty of women.

James Henry Green Collection, 1920s

OLD RED KAREN WOMAN
A Kayah village woman wearing
the traditional red shawl.

James Henry Green Collection, 1920s

The early Mons founded a kingdom called
Suvannabhumi or 'the Golden Land', which is
known to modern-day Mons as Hongsawatoi.
This represented a loose federation of three states,
Haripunjaya in what is now northern Thailand,
Dvaravati further to the south, and around
Thaton, the ancient capital of what is today still
part of the Mon State.

From the Martaban coast, the Mons made trading
and cultural contacts with the civilisations of
India and Ceylon, from where Buddhism was first
introduced. In the ninth century the great Mon
city of Pegu was founded. Originally known as
'Hamsavarti', the *hamsa* or goose is the mount
of Brahma in the Indian tradition, and even
today the flying goose is the emblem of Mon
nationalists. Raised on a tall pole, it also marks
out Mon Buddhist temples. Over the centuries, the
migrations of Burmans and other ethnic groups

began to pressure Mon civilisation. Although
Mons continued to rule much of Lower Burma
for around a thousand years, their kingdoms
gradually fell: Thaton to the Burmans, Dvaravati
to the Khmers and Haripunjaya to the Tai-Shans.
In the west Mon kingdoms survived, but in 1757
independence was finally lost when the great
Burman monarch, Alaunghpaya, crushed the
uprising of the last Mon ruler, Smin Dhaw.

The British initially considered supporting Mons
against the Burmans when they annexed the
country in the nineteenth century, but eventually
chose Burmese as the official language of
government. This was to have a devastating effect
on Mon culture and, within two generations,
many areas had lost all traces of their Mon
history. Despite its important place in Burmese
cultures, the Mon language is rarely taught
beyond primary level in government schools even

UNTITLED
An unrecorded group of tribal
women in the mountains of north
Burma.

James Henry Green Collection, 1920s

today. Only in rural villages is it still taught by
Buddhist monks and teachers, and its revival is a
main platform of all Mon nationalists.

The Mons are traditionally lowlanders, who raise
cattle and cultivate rice and vegetables. Mon
villages are typically large and contain houses,
granaries, cattle sheds and a monastery, which
serves as a school, and an image house containing
statues of the Buddha. By contrast, their distant
hill relations, the Palaungs, cultivate tea, while
the Was, another related group, have subsisted on
slash-and-burn agriculture and hunting. However,
the historic relationship between these different
peoples is not at all apparent, except in a few
aspects of language.

Theravada Buddhism is the major element of Mon
culture which has also been absorbed into Burman
culture. Buddhist monks play a central role in the

lives of all Mon communities. There is also a
sisterhood of nuns – the *prea min* – who have an
inferior status in the monastic order. As well as
officiating at weddings and funerals, Mon
monks are often called on for advice about the
supernatural and sometimes act as astrologers.

As in other Buddhist communities in Burma,
traditional religions or practices also survive.
Male and female shamans are often consulted
about public and private matters, for which they
are paid a small fee. The shamans also lead spirit
dances – during which they are said to be
possessed by spirits – at annual festivals to
appease local spirits or at private houses, where
they are thought to alleviate the effects of an
illness or disaster in a family.

The Mons also have interesting traditions
surrounding childbirth. Immediately after the

**FOUR ARAKANESE WOMEN
POUNDING RICE**
Unidentified women, presumed to
be Chins from Arakan State.

James Henry Green Collection, 1920s

birth, the mother and baby are bathed and smeared with turmeric mixed with water. The baby's shoulder and hip joints are set, as the Mons believe that they are not properly set in place at birth. For the three days after the birth, the mother must rest near a special fire while hot stones are applied to her body.

ETHNIC GROUPS OF ARAKAN STATE

Arakan (or Rakhine) State is situated west of Chin State, bordering Bangladesh and the Bay of Bengal in north-west Burma. The great Arakan Yoma range of mountains separating the territory from the central Irrawaddy River plains historically left Arakan isolated from the rest of the country and encouraged closer links with north-east India and what has become modern-day Bangladesh.

The ethnic origins of Arakan's estimated 3 million inhabitants are much disputed. Some anthropologists believe the majority *Rakhine* are Burmans with Indian ancestry or Indians with Burman characteristics, whereas Rakhine nationalists claim that they are a separate race. According to one legend, the first inhabitants of the region were a dark-skinned people known as the Bilu – meaning 'ogre' in Burmese – and the name of the state probably derives from a corruption of the Pali name, Rakkhapura, which means 'land of the ogres'.

Later migrants from the eastern Indian sub-continent developed Hindu-Buddhist kingdoms in the region before the first millennium. These included the kingdom of Dinnyawaddy around the first century AD, where the sacred Mahamuni Buddha image was first cast. Although speaking a dialect similar to Burman migrants who entered Burma around the same time, the Rakhines maintained an independent kingdom and kept their own chronicles and histories, listing more than a hundred kings who, it was claimed, ruled for over three thousand years in all.

The first capital emerged at Vesali, but it was later superceded by Mrauk-U (Myohaung) nearby, where the royal court survived until the Burman invasion of 1784 when the Mahamuni Buddha image – the symbol of Arakan's independence – was captured and transported away to Mandalay, where it remains today.

The majority Rakhines are thus thought to be the first of the modern-day settlers in Arakan, along with the *Khami* (Mro), who are Chin-related hill peoples (see below) that claim to have arrived over a thousand years ago. The *Maramagyi* say they came to Arakan from India in the fifth century as traders and stayed in Mrauk-U, while the *Thet* (Shakama) came from what is now Bangladesh, along with the *Daignet* (another Chin-related group), who are said to have fled to Arakan State to escape fighting in Bengal to the west during the fifteenth to seventeenth centuries.

Arakan was also strongly influenced by Portuguese and Dutch trading contacts before the British annexation in 1825, but the most controversial association today is with its Muslim neighbours. Islamic influence in Arakan dates back centuries, both through Arab merchants and also through Muslim settlers from neighbouring Chittagong, where many Rakhines once lived. A great movement of peoples, however, has taken place in the northern border areas, which began

A CAMHOW CHIN GIRL, CARRYING BASKET
Over forty sub-groups of Chin live in Burma's north-west mountains.

James Henry Green Collection, 1920s

with the upheavals of the Second World War. An estimated quarter of the population of Arakan (renamed Rakhine State in 1974) are Muslims today, but twice in the past twenty years a mass exodus of over 250,000 Muslim refugees – known as *Rohingyas* – has taken place into Bangladesh, with Muslim families complaining of official harassment by the authorities.

Small Muslim and Rakhine insurgent groups continue to operate in the borderland mountains, but since 1988 the SLORC government has slowly begun to open up the state to foreign visitors. The major industry is fishing, with Arakan having the third-largest fishery site in Burma. Four major rivers, the Kaladan, Lemyo, Mayu and Naaf, irrigate the extensive lowland rice fields in the north, while opium is sometimes cultivated in remote hill regions.

CHIN STATE

The *Chin* occupy a vast mountain range which runs up the north-western side of Burma into north-east India. The region is sparsely populated – there are thought to be a million and a half Chins in Burma – and the difficult terrain has inhibited development, communications and transport in the region.

The Chins (or Zomis as they call themselves) have a Tibeto-Burman ancestry and share many aspects of their culture and language with the Zo peoples in the neighbouring Indian state of Mizoram. People speaking Chin-related languages live in much of north-west Burma, north-east India and south-east Bangladesh. Some scholars believe that Chins had reached the lowland plains in Burma as early as the middle of the first millennium AD. Their subsequent migrations westwards into the mountains were the result of fighting and power struggles between different Burman, Shan and Mon rulers after the thirteenth century.

Some scholars have speculated that the name Chin is an Anglicised version of a Burmese inscription word for the Chins meaning 'friend', but Chin historians, who prefer to use their own name Zo, say that it comes from the Burmese word for 'basket'. When Burmans entered north-west Burma they discovered a people carrying baskets, so they called the local river the Chindwin ('valley of the baskets') and the people they named the Chins. But certainly, the Chins have long been in contact with Burman lowlanders and neighbouring Indians, mainly for trading links.

More than forty Chin or Zo sub-groups have been identified by anthropologists in Burma alone, including the Asho, Chin Bok, Chin Bon and Laytoo, many of which are distinguished by unique costumes or tattoos. Traditional Chin groups also live in the borderlands of Arakan State, such as the Daignet and Khami.

Most of the terrain occupied by Chins is mountainous, and settlements are generally found between 3,000 and 7,000 feet, where the people lives by slash-and-burn agriculture. They are also skilled hunters and animal sacrifice plays an important role in animistic ceremonies. Hill Chins have long depended on other ethnic groups, particularly lowland peoples such as the Burmans, for certain products, most notably metals. They also trade cloth, beeswax and other forest products.

Chin women have traditionally participated in all tasks in the village, except blacksmithing, house-building and clearing the forest for planting. Most Chin men are monogamous and, while polygamy was historically permitted, it was generally only

SUNSET LAKE INLE
Inle Lake in south-west Shan State
is home to the Intha people, who
make their living on the waters.

James Henry Green Collection, 1920s

CHIN PAKOKKU (1890)
A group of Chins who had come
down to the plains near Pakokku.

*British Library/Oriental and India
Office Collection*

LEG ROWERS LAKE INLE
Intha leg rowers have gained world renown
for their unique method of propelling boats.

*James Henry Green Collection, 1920s
British Library/OIOC (overleaf)*

practised by wealthy commoners and aristocrats – the two social classes into which northern Chin society is stratified. Among the southern Chins, individual families earn their high status by providing great feasts for the community, gaining them merit.

Although some Chins retain their animist or traditional spirit religions, a majority of Chins began converting to Christianity at the end of the nineteenth century, when British and American Protestant missionaries began work on both sides of the India–Burma border.

Many Chins also joined the British army and served with distinction during the Second World War. Under the British, however, nationalist leaders were frustrated by the division of Chin peoples between north-east India and Burma. Inside Burma, too, there has been continuing

dissension. Until the introduction of the 1974 constitution, the Chins were denied even a state.

The Chin State has not been affected by ethnic violence or armed conflict to the same degree as most other minority regions of the country. However it remains very impoverished and undeveloped. In the late 1980s an armed movement known as the Chin National Front sprang up in the northern border area with India. As a result, much of Chin State has remained off-limits to outsiders.

The goal of many Chin and Mizo leaders is to create a sovereign 'Zo' land, divided into the states of East Zoram, encompassing Chin State in Burma; West Zoram, covering part of south-eastern Bangladesh plus Tripura in India; Central Zoram, consisting of Mizoram; and North Zoram, which covers Manipur in India.

NAGA

The Patkai Range in north Burma is home to the country's estimated 100,000 *Naga,* another sub-group of the Tibeto-Burman people. The majority of Nagas, possibly more than one million, live across the border in India, where a political movement has been fighting for the establishment of an independent Nagaland since the early 1950s. This conflict has spread into Burma, where there has often been heavy fighting, pushing villages deeper into the hills. Historically, Nagas were unrecognised on Burma's political map, but the SLORC is now considering the establishment of a Naga 'self-administered zone' under Burma's new constitution.

The traditions and legends of the Nagas trace the course of their migrations. For centuries, the different Naga clans and peoples have been fighting among themselves and other peoples in their region. At the beginning of the thirteenth century, the Shan chief Sukhapa subjugated the Nagas, treating them poorly, while their dealings with the Ahom kings of Assam fluctuated between hostility and friendliness in the sixteenth century. In 1832–3, the King of Manipur marched through Naga territory and established some control over the region. Under the British, a further attempt was made to bring them under outside control, with inter-village raids and head-hunting expeditions being stamped out in the administered area.

The derivation of the name Naga is not clear; some scholars believe it comes from the Sanskrit word *naga,* meaning 'mountain', whereas others claim it comes from the word *nok,* which means 'people' in some Tibeto-Burman languages. Until recently, the groups would call themselves by individual names, such as the Htangan, Pyengoo, Haimi and Rangpan in Burma, and the Konyak, Ao, Sema and Angami in India. Increased contact among groups fighting for an independent homeland has, however, led most to unify under the common name of Naga in recent decades.

Nagas traditionally build their villages on the summit of a hill or spur running off a mountain range, 3,000–4,000 feet above sea level. This type of location was sought primarily for defence purposes, and villages often had a protective stone wall, dyke or fence. The Nagas traditionally practised shifting cultivation, although their villages are permanent. Herding, hunting and fishing are also practised. Most Nagas enjoy hunting as a sport as well as a means of obtaining meat. They hunt tigers, leopards and wild boar with guns and spears, aided by dogs. Traps are used for small animals and birds, but the hunting of elephants in pitfalls has long been outlawed.

For centuries, Nagas have been isolated due to poor communications in their rugged land. This, together with inter-village and inter-group feuds, has made them self-reliant and not dependent on trade, although they will exchange cloth, baskets and carved goods for special items which they cannot find in their homelands. Weaving is one of the most important industries for the Nagas and their cloth is famous throughout Burma for its variety of colour and design. In many villages, home-grown cotton is used, although thread is often imported from India.

Every Naga village traditionally contains a *morung,* a sleeping place for unmarried men, who go there as boys from the age of six or seven. Unmarried boys and girls work together for long periods in the fields and premarital relations are not frowned upon. Young people are free to choose their marriage partner, although a bride price is common.

VIEW OF NSOP THROUGH TREES FROM THE SOUTH
A typical river valley scene in Upper Burma.

James Henry Green Collection, 1920s

Although some Nagas in Burma and India have converted to Christianity, their indigenous religion is still strong. Almost all traditional religious ceremonies are designed to protect and increase crops. Nagas proscribe many activities on certain days on religious grounds; the most important ceremony is the individual or village *genna* during which work and contact with the outside world are avoided. *Gennas* may also be held to ensure the health of a community or peaceful relations between neighbouring communities. Some Nagas believe that good souls go to a place towards the sunrise, while evil souls are destined for a terrible place in the direction of the sunset.

VALLEY IN UPPER BURMA
The myriad valleys of Burma provided the conduits for early migrations.

British Library/Oriental and India Office Collection

BURMAN

The central plains of Burma are the traditional home of the *Burman*, the largest ethnic group in the country. They comprise around two-thirds of the population and are of Tibeto-Burman descent. There are references to Burmans inhabiting the country towards the end of the first millennium AD, and some anthropologists believe that they first appeared in the Mandalay area in the ninth century and then expanded south, south-west and north over the next two centuries.

As they pushed south into Burma, the early Burman migrants appeared to absorb another Tibeto-Burman group, the Pyu, who occupied the central Irrawaddy valley and left important monuments at Sri Ksetra. Still further to the south was another regional power, the Mons, and for centuries Lower Burma became a battleground between different Burman and Mon rulers as they vied for supremacy, each building great royal capitals throughout the country.

The Burmans' greatest capital was at Pagan on the banks of the River Irrawaddy, a site chosen for its strategic and mystical significance. It was from here that the great King Anawrahta launched his attack on the Mon capital at Thaton in the eleventh century, seizing monks who introduced both writing and Buddhist religion to their captors.

There followed a golden period in Burma's history, and subsequent dynasties extended their territory into Laos, Siam and north-east India. The city of Pagan was sacked by the Mongol armies of Kublai Khan in 1287, but later capitals were established at Toungoo, Ava, Sagaing, Amarapura and Mandalay.

In the following centuries wars continued with different Chinese, Shan, Mon and Rakhine rulers. Many of the opposing forces were multi-ethnic, and these were not wars fought on strictly ethnic lines. But in the second half of the eighteenth century, a death blow was finally dealt to Mon dreams of independence by the powerful Burman leader Alaunghpaya, who in 1753 drove the Mons from Ava. Within four years of his capture of Ava, the Mon capital at Pegu had fallen to his troops. Three decades later, the Rakhine kingdom was also toppled. At the same time, ethnic Burmans also began to move into Tenasserim, where related Tavoyans had long lived.

The British annexed Burma in three wars between 1825 and 1886, but this did not halt Burman expansion. Under the British occupation, many Burmans began to settle in the Irrawaddy and Sittang deltas, where they cultivated rice on an extensive scale for export. Burmans typically lived – often as today – in small settlements running alongside a river or road surrounded by garden land, rice fields, a monastery and a cemetery. Almost every village had a rest house and pagoda and small spirit houses usually located under trees. Houses were wooden and raised above the ground, with a front verandah to receive guests and a rear verandah for cooking and washing. In a two-storey house, custom dictated that a woman was not allowed to sleep above a man.

For sixty years, Burma was under British control, mostly as a province of India. The British established a two-tier system of administration: 'Ministerial Burma' which was dominated by the majority population of Burmans and the 'Frontier Areas' where the ethnic minorities lived. In 1948, after a brief period of rule by Imperial Japan, Burma gained independence and the country was finally unified. Burmese was the official language and, although some ethnic minority ministers were appointed to the early cabinets, ethnic Burmans have, in the main, come to dominate government politics in the new Union of Burma. The armed insurgencies which have since continued in many ethnic minority areas are just one consequence of this.

Burman culture, however, has itself continued to absorb many influences. The Burman royal courts had contact with the Portuguese, French and British as early as the sixteenth century, and the country saw an influx of Chinese and Indian immigrants in the nineteenth and twentieth centuries. Dating back many more centuries, elements of Chinese and Indian culture have also been adopted, including language, dress, food, implements, medicine, art, architecture and politics. Influences have been absorbed, too, from other ethnic groups – notably the Buddhist Mons and Shans – and these have all blended together to produce the diversity of cultural expression that exists in Burma today.

However, some of the ancient Burman court culture has survived on its own. This includes classical dance dramas – known as *yodaya zat* – which were thought to be passed on by Thai prisoners captured by King Hsinbyushin in the late 1700s, and marionette theatre – *yok-thei-pwe* – which was developed during the reign of King Bagyidaw in the early nineteenth century. Marionette theatre was the forerunner to *zat-pwe* or actors' theatre, which was popular until the

ATSIS ROOFING HOUSE
Building houses is a job with which all hill villagers help, such as these Azis in Kachin State.

James Henry Green Collection, 1920s

advent of cinema in the 1930s. Classical music was also adopted from Thai prisoners under King Hsinbyushin, although there is an older stratum of vocal folk music. *Pwes,* or street theatre, are an everyday part of Burmese life and have a long history. Dramas are performed in the open air at religious festivals, weddings, funerals, ordination ceremonies and sporting events. The performances can be anything from slapstick comedy and dancing to serious drama.

Perhaps the greatest testament to both Burman and multi-ethnic 'Burmese' culture is the great Shwedagon Pagoda in Rangoon, which rises 326 feet above the city skyline. Revered by all Buddhists and in an area originally inhabited by Mons, the Shwedagon dates back 2,500 years. Its glittering gold stupa stands on a terraced base and is covered with 60 tonnes of gold leaf. The gilded crown – or *hti* – is studded with more than 5,000 diamonds, 1,000 gold bells and 400 silver bells which tinkle when the wind stirs. At the very top of the *hti* is a gold cask which contains a massive 76-carat diamond, which Kipling famously named a 'winking wonder'.

The legend surrounding the Shwedagon Pagoda refers to two merchants who travelled to India, where they met the Buddha under the sacred *bodhi* tree. They offered to share the food they had for the journey – honey and cakes – and in return, the Buddha gave them eight sacred hairs from his head. On their way home, the merchants gave away four of the hairs to kings they encountered, but the remaining four were presented to the Burman King Okkalapa in Dagon (the ancient site of Rangoon). The king enshrined them on the city's holy Singuttara Hill. Legend contends that when it was excavated centuries later, the cask miraculously contained all eight of the Buddha's hairs.

Much of the historical and political information in the above account is extracted from: Martin Smith, *Ethnic Groups in Burma: Development, Democracy and Human Rights* (Anti-Slavery International, London, 1994) and Martin Smith, *Burma: Insurgency and the Politics of Ethnicity* (Zed Books, London and New Jersey,1991).The ethnographical information is largely based on classifications in F. Lebar, G. Hickey and J. Musgrave (eds.), *Ethnic Groups of Mainland South-East Asia (*Human Relations Areas File, New Haven, 1964).

HKAHKU GIRL TAPPING OPIUM
In British days, as today, opium was grown by shifting cultivation in Burma's mountain borderlands.

James Henry Green Collection, 1920s

James Henry Green (1893–1975)

Much of the early anthropology of places remote from the European hub was written by amateurs who were in the region for reasons of Empire: administrative, military or missionary. James Henry Green was an officer whose appointment to the Indian Army took him to Burma in 1918. He remained there for twenty years, spending much of his time in the remote hill regions. His work took him to places previously unmapped by Europeans and his fascination with the people he met developed into a lifelong pursuit of anthropology, consolidated in his Fellowship of the Royal Anthropological Institute from 1928. His observations became the basis of a dissertation submitted to the Anthropology Department of Cambridge University in 1934, The tribes of Upper Burma north of 24 latitude and their classification.

In this text, and in his other writings, Green's fascination with ethnic difference in the hill regions is a motivating force. He studied the nuances of different customs, beliefs, languages and physical attributes which distinguished neighbouring groups and recorded these according to the anthropological theories of the day. However, his was not a purely clinical appraisal of ethnicity; Green's personal interest and empathy are evident in his collection of over 1500 photographs, which provide a rare insight into Burma of the 1920s.

After Green's death in 1975, a trust was established in his name, to ensure the care of his textile and photographic collections. In 1992 his archive was transferred to Brighton Museum and a research centre, The Green Centre for the study of Non-Western Art, was established. A publication on James Henry Green's archive is in preparation.
Dr Elizabeth Dell, Green Centre for Non-Western Art

Sir (James) George Scott (1851–1935)

Sir J. G. Scott's name will always be associated with Burma in his capacity as a colonial officer and for his writings on the history and lives of its people.

Scott first visited the Far East as a correspondent for the 'Standard' in 1875 and went on to Burma where he became headmaster of St John's College, Rangoon. While in Rangoon he wrote letters to the Daily News *as 'Our Special Correspondent' on the political troubles in Upper Burma. In 1882, his two-volume work,* The Burman, his Life and Notions, *was published under the pseudonym, Shway Yoe. The book was a sympathetic study of Burmese society and culture at a time of great change.*

After Burma was assimilated into the Indian Empire in 1886, Scott joined the Burma Commission and became a valued administrator in the turbulent Shan States. His later works include The Upper Burma Gazetteer *(5 vols), 1901;* Burma, a Handbook, *1906; and* Burma and Beyond: A Ragbag of Races, *1932.*
Rod Hamilton, British Library/OIOC

BIBLIOGRAPHY

Allott, A. J. *Inked Over, Ripped Out*, Pen American Center, New York, 1993

Amnesty International *Myanmar: 'No law at all': Human rights violations under military rule*, London, 1992

Asia Watch *A Modern Form of Slavery: Trafficking of Burmese Women and Girls into Brothels in Thailand*, New York, 1993

Aung, M. H. *Folk Elements in Burmese Buddhism*, Oxford, 1962

A History of Burma, Columbia University Press, 1967

Aung San Suu Kyi *Freedom from Fear*, Penguin, London, 1991

Aung Thwin, M *Pagan: The Origins of Modern Burma*, Univ. of Hawaii Press, 1985

Bailey, Sir H. *Journal of the Royal Asiatic Society* (Parts 1–2), London, 1996

Bareights, A. *Les Lahtu – Contribution à L'étude de L'organisation Sociale D'une Ethnie Chin de Haute-Birmanie*, Selaf, Paris, 1981

Barua, S. N. and Surenda Nath *Tribes of the Indo-Burman Border, a Sociological History of the Inhabitants of the Patkai Range*, 1991

Becker, S. *The Blue-Eyed Shan Sphere*, London, 1984

Bharadwaji, L. *A History of Burma*, Rangoon, 1951

Bisch, J. *Why Buddha Smiles*, Collins, London, 1964

Boucaud, Louis and André *Burma's Golden Triangle*, Asia Books, Bangkok, 1985

Bunge, F. M. *Burma, A Country Study*, Dept of the Army, USA, 1983

Byles, M. *Journey into Burmese Silence*, Allen & Unwin, London, 1962

Cambell, Pongnoi, Voraphitak (eds.) *From the Hands of the Hills*, Hong Kong, 1978

Carrapiett, W. J. S. *Kachin Tribes of Burma*, Rangoon, 1929

Chaturabhand, P. *People of the Hills*, Duang Kamol, Bangkok, 1980

Chit, K. M. *Burmese Legends*, Tamarind Press, Bangkok, 1984

Collis, Maurice *She was a Queen*, Faber & Faber, London, 1936

The Outward Journey, Faber & Faber, London, 1952

Into Hidden Burma, Faber & Faber, London, 1953

Marco Polo, Faber & Faber, London, 1959

Colquhoun, A. R. *Amongst the Shans*, Field & Tuer, London, 1885

Crossroads: Centre for S.E. Asia Asian Studies, Special Burma Studies Issue, Northern Illinois Univ., 1988

Durrenberger, E. P. *Lisu Religion*, Center for Southeast Asian Studies, Northern Illinois Univ., 1989

Enriquez, C. M. *A Burmese Arcady*, London, 1923

The Races of Burma, Handbooks for the Indian Army, India, 1933

Falla, J. *True Love and Bartholemew: Rebels on the Burmese Border*, Cambridge Univ. Press, Cambridge, 1991

Fryer, F. W. R. *Tribes on the Frontier of Burma*, 1907

Fuerer-Haimendorf, C. von *The Naked Nagas*, Methuen & Co, London, 1939

George, E. C. S. *Burma Gazetteer* (Vol. A), Ruby Mines District, Rangoon, reprint 1962

Golish, V de *Au Pays des Femmes de Girafes*, Arthaud, Grenoble, 1958

Grontham, S. G. *Burma Gazetteer*, Tharrawaddy District Vol. A, Rangoon, reprint 1959

Grose, F. S. *Tribes of the Shan States*, Mandalay, 1922

Grunfeld, F. V. *Wayfarers of the Thai Forest*, Time/Life Books (The Akha), 1982

Guillon, E. *Notes sur le Bouddhisme Môn*, Vandenhoech & Ruprecht, Göttingen, 1983

Hall, G. L. *Golden Boats from Burma*, Macrae Smith Co., USA, 1961

Hammerton, J. A. (ed.), *Tribes, Races and Cultures of India and neighbouring countries*, Mittal Publications, Delhi, 1984

Hannay, S. F. 'Sketch of Singhpos', *Journal of the Asiatic Society*, 1837

Harvey, G. E. *Outline of History*, Longmans and Green, India, 1926

Hertz, W. A. *Burma Gazetteer, Myitkyina District*, Rangoon, 1912, reprint 1960

Hodson, T. C. *The Naga Tribes of Manipur*, Macmillan & Co., London, 1911

Hoefer, H. J. *Burma*, APA Productions, Insight Guides, Hong Kong, 1981

Horam, M. M. *Nagas, Old Ways and New Trends*, Cosmo Publications, New Delhi, 1988

Hutton, J. H. *The Angami Nagas*, Macmillan & Co., London, 1921

The Sema Nagas, Macmillan & Co., London, 1921

Kapp, R. A. *The Journal of Asian Studies Vol. 38 No 4*, Association of Asian Studies, USA, 1979

Khaing, Mi Mi *Burmese Family*, Longmans & Green Co. London, 1946

Lathan, Ronald *Marco Polo: The Travels of Marco Polo*, Penguin, London, 1958

Leach, E. R. *Political Systems of Highland Burma*, Beacon Press, USA, 1954

Lebar, F., G. Hickey and J. Musgrave (eds.) *Ethnic Groups of Mainland South-East Asia*, Human Relations Areas File, New Haven, 1964

Lee, C. Y. *The Sawbwa and his Secretary*, Farrar Straus & Cudahy, New York, 1958

Lehman, F. K. *The Structure of Chin Society*, Univ. of Illinois Press, 1963

'Burma: Kayah Society as a Function of the Shan-Burma-Karen Context', in J. Steward (ed.), *Contemporary Change in Traditional Societies*, Univ. of Illinois, 1967

Lewis, Norman *A Dragon Apparent*, Eland Books, London, reprint 1982

Golden Earth, Eland Books, London, reprint 1983

Lewis, Paul and Elaine *Peoples of the Golden Triangle*, Thames & Hudson, 1984

Lintner, Bertil *Outrage*, Review Publishing, Hong Kong, 1989

Land of Jade, White Lotus Books, Bangkok, 1990

Aung San Suu Kyi and Burma's Unfinished Renaissance, White Lotus Books, Bangkok, 1991

Burma in Revolt, Opium and Insurgency Since 1948, Westview Press, 1994

Lowis, C. C. *The Tribes of Burma* Ethnographic Survey of India, Rangoon, 1919

Mannin, E. *Land of the Crested Lion*, Travel Book Club, London, 1954

Marshall, Rev. H. I. *The Karen People of Burma*, Univ. of Columbia Press, 1992

Minority Rights Group, *India: The Nagas and the North-East*, London, 1980

Mirante, E. T. *Burmese Looking Glass: A Human Rights Adventure and a Jungle Revolution*, Grove Press, New York, 1993

Moore, R. W. 'Burma's Hills Flash with Color', *National Geographic*, October 1931

'Burma', *National Geographic*, February 1963

Mottin, J. *Contes et Légendes Hmong Blanc*, Don Bosco Press, Bangkok, 1980

History of the Hmong, Odeon Store, Bangkok, 1980

Myint, Daw Ni Ni *Burma's Struggle Against British Imperialism*, Universities Press, Rangoon, 1983

Myint, Thein Pe. *The Beginning of History in the Chin Division*, Rangoon Information Department (Burmese), 1967

Naing, Min. *The Dance Variety of the Union of Burma*, Ministry of Culture (Burmese), 1959

Palaungs of Burma, Ministry of Culture,

Rangoon, Burma, 1960
Races of Burma, Ministry of Culture, Rangoon, Burma, 1960
Traditional Festivals of the Kayan, Ministry of Culture (Burmese), 1961
Nash, M. *The Golden Road to Modernity*, University of Chicago, Wiley & Sons, New York, 1965
Nassif, R. *U Thant in New York*, Hurst, London, 1988
O'Brien, H. *Forgotten Land*, Michael Joseph, London, 1991
O'Connor, V. C. S. *The Silken East* (vols. 1, 2), Hutchinson & Co., London, 1904
Mandalay and other cities in Burma, Hutchinson & Co., London, 1907
Oo, Sein Hla *The Opium Manual*, Rangoon, Burma, reprint 1964
Page, A. J. *Burma Gazetteer*, Pegu District, Rangoon, 1917
Pfanmuller, Klein *Burma the Golden*, APA Productions, Hong Kong, 1982
Po, Dr San C *Burma and the Karens*, Elliot Stock, London, 1928
Rodrigue, Y. *Nat-Pwe: Burma's Supernatural Sub-Culture*, Kiscadale, 1992
Saung Aye *Burma in the Back Row*, Asia 2000, Hong Kong, 1989
Scott, Sir J. G. *Gazetteer of Upper Burma and Shan States*, Rangoon, 1900
A Handbook of Practical Information, David O'Connor, 1921
'The Hill Tribes of Burma', *National Geographic*, March 1922
(1963 reprint Shway Yoe) *The Burman His Life and Notions*, Norton, New York, USA
Seagrave, G. *Burma Surgeon*, Norton & Co. New York, 1943
Seidenfaden, E. *The Thai Peoples*, Siam Society, Bangkok, Thailand, 1958
Shwe Lu Maung, *Burma: Nationalism and Ideology*, Dhaka Univ. Press, Dhaka, 1989
Silverstein, J, *Burmese Politics, The Dilemma of National Unity*, Rutgers Univ. Press, New Brunswick, 1990
Smith, A.W. 'Working Teak in the Burma Forests', *National Geographic*, August 1930
Smith, Martin *Ethnic Groups in Burma: Development, Democracy and Human Rights*, Anti-Slavery International, London, 1994
Burma: Insurgency and the Politics of Ethnicity, Zed Books, London and New Jersey, 1991
Smith, N. *Burma Road*, Garden City Publishing, New York, 1940
Spiro, M. *Burmese Supernaturalism*, Prentice/Hall, USA, 1967
Steinburg, David I. *The Future of Burma*, The Asia Society, University Press of America, USA, 1990
Stevenson, H. N. C. *The Economics of the Central Chin Tribes*, Times of India Press, Bombay, 1943
The Hill People of Burma, Burma Pamphlets No. 6, Calcutta, 1944
Strachan, P. *Pagan*, Kiscadale Publishing, Singapore, 1989
Taik, A. A. *Visions of Shwedagon*, White Lotus, Bangkok, Thailand, 1989
Taw Sein, K. O. *Kalyani Inscriptions*, Government Printing, Rangoon, 1892
Taylor, R. H. *An Undeveloped State, The Study of Modern Burma's Politics*, Monash University, Australia, 1983
The State in Burma, C. Hurst, London, 1987
Tegenfeldt, H.G. *A Century of Growth: The Kachin Baptist Church of Burma*, William Carey Library, California, 1974
Temple, Sir R. C. *The Thirty-seven Nats*, London, 1906
Thanegi, Ma *The Illusion of Life: Burmese Marionettes*, White Orchid Press, 1994
Thaw, Aung *Historical Sights in Burma*, Ministry of Culture, Rangoon, 1972
Thcin, M. M. *Burmese Folk Songs*, The Asoka Society, Oxford, 1970
Tu, Mya M. (various authors) *The Tarons of Burma*, Special Report Series, No. 1, Rangoon, 1966
Tun Shwe, Khine, *A Guide to Mrauk-U, An Ancient City of Rakhine*, Myanmar, 1993
Vumson *Zo History*, Aizawl, Mizoram, 1986
White, Sir H. T. *A Civil Servant in Burma*, Arnold, London, 1913
Yang, B. O. *Golden Triangle Frontier and Wilderness*, Joint Publishing, Hong Kong, 1987
Yawnghwe, Chao Tzang *The Shan of Burma: Memoirs of an Exile*, Institute of Southeast Asian Studies, Singapore, 1987

GLOSSARY OF COMMON NAMES AND ALTERNATIVES

THE terminology for many common names in Burma is confusing, especially when transliterated into English. Since 1989, the SLORC government has also changed many official names, including the name of the country, from Burma to Myanmar. In particular, the terms Burman and Burmese are often ambiguous and sometimes are used interchangeably. Generally, however, Burman is used to denote the majority ethnic group, while Burmese is an adjective, denoting, for example, language or citizenship. This means that somebody may be an ethnic Shan, Kachin or Mon but, at the same time, can also be a Burmese citizen.

Akha	Kaw	Lahta	Zayein
Akyab	Sittwe	Lahu	Muser
Arakan	Rakhine	Maymyo	Pyin U Lwin
Ava	Inwa	Mergui	Myeik
Bassein	Pathein	Moulmein	Mawlamyine
Bre	Kayaw	Mrauk-U	Myohaung
Burma	Myanmar	Pagan	Bagan
Burman	Bama	Pa-O	Taungthu
Burmese	Bamar	Pegu	Bago
Chin	Zomi	Prome	Pyay
Hmong	Meo	Rangoon	Yangon
Irrawaddy	Ayeyarwady	Salween	Thanlwin
Kachin	Wunpawng	Shan	Tai
Karen	Kayin	Ta-ang	Palaung
Kayan	Padaung	Tavoy	Dawei
Khami	Mro	Tenasserim	Tanintharyi

A leg rower on Lake Inle
in Shan State

ACKNOWLEDGEMENTS

First, I would like to thank my parents, Edward and Dorothy Diran, for encouraging me to travel and to absorb foreign cultures at an early age. Also to my wife's mother, Yoshiko Teramoto, who supported me in the completion of the project. To Skip 'Wizard' Whitney for his kind encouragement, and to my literary agent, Susan Wakeford, for her advice. To Michael Dover at Weidenfeld & Nicolson who guided me, to Dr Melanie Chew for her comments and to Ian Hewitson for his maps. Special thanks to Charles Hardeman who 'smacked' me one night in a bar to make me realise the importance of my work and then made good his commitment and promise to see that the book was published.

Thanks, too, to all my friends in Burma who have helped me on my journey, and to the tribal people of Burma who have always been generous and have opened my eyes to the dignity and exquisite humanity of their lives.

Lastly, thanks to my wife, Junko, who has stuck with me throughout it all, supporting my dream for so many years.

Thank you all.

Richard K. Diran
Bangkok, 1997

dress and jewellery, 32, **33**
homeland and origins, 32, 201
Lashio, 198
Leach, Edmund, 199
Lisu
  dress and jewellery, **65–71**
  graves, **207**
  homeland and origins, 64, 201,
    206, 208, 209
  language, 208
  religion, 209
  villages, **207**, 208
Loikaw, 9
Lowis, C. C., 160

Mali Hka River, 14, 20, 28, 201
Man, *see* Yao
Mandalay, 196, 231
Maramagyi, 160, **163**, 225
Maran clan, 26, 202
Marip clan, 26, 202
marriage and courtship customs
  arranged marriages, 202, 220
  bride price, 202, 208, 212, 220,
    230
  courtship dances, 211
  Hmong, 208
  Kachin, 202
  Lahta, 219–20
  Padaung, 136, 210
  pre-marital sex, 180, 212, 230
  Shan, 205–6
  spring festival, 209
Martaban, 154
Maru, 26, 200, 201
  dog traders, **204**
  dress and jewellery, **29–31, 203**
  homeland and origins, 26
  language, 28
Mayao, *see* Hmong
Maymyo, 198
Meo, *see* Hmong
Mien, *see* Yao
Mindon, King, 216
mineral and gem deposits, 8
Minoo-Minaw, 132
Mon
  ancient cities and rulers, 154,
    196, 223–4
  art and culture, 154, 223
  Buddhist tradition, 154
  dominated by Burmans, 11, 182
  dress and jewellery, **158–9**
  homeland and origins, 154, 196,
    222–3
  Hongsawatoi (Suvannabhumi),
    223
  New Mon State Party, 222
  population numbers, 199
  refugees, 222
  religion, 223
Mon-Khmer, 154, 196, 222
Mon State, 222–5
Mong Tai Army, 204
Mount Popa, **191**
Mrauk-U (Myohaung), 160, 225
Mro, *see* Khami
Myawaddy, 195

Naga
  bachelor houses (morung), 177,
    230
  dress and jewellery, **173–81**
  gennas (village ceremonies), 231
  head-hunters, 11, 172
  homeland and origins, 8, 172,
    230
  isolation of, 11, 230
  nationalism, 230

religion, 231
  war dance, **177**
names in Burma, 12, 236
Narapatisithu, King, 112, 214
Narathu, King, 190
Nat (Nat-pwe) festival, 187
National Geographic, 7, 132
National League for Democracy, 8
Ne Win, General, 7, 34, 204, 209
N'hKhum clan, 26, 202
Ninggawn Wa, 202
N'Mai River, 14, 20, 26, 28, 32
Nsop, **230**
Nung-Rawang
  dress, **23–5, 200, 201**
  homeland and origins, 22, 201
  language, 200
  pygmies, 22

opium trade, 11, **11**, 101, 201
  addicts, 212
  cash crop, 114, 215
  cultivation, 55, 207–8, 208–9,
    233
  encouraged by Kuomintang, 204
  financing opposition groups, 54
  Golden Triangle, 54
  independent warlords, **48**, 54,
    204–5
  and Shan insurrection, 204–5
  smoking, **56–61**
  weights, **59**

Pa-O
  absorbing neighbours, 10
  agriculture, 210, **211**
  dress and jewellery, **77–9, 210**
  homeland and origins, 76, 210
  insurrection, 210
  language, 126
  National Organisation, 144
  religion, 210
  uprising, 204
Padaung
  agriculture, 219
  dress and neck coils, 7, 11,
    137–43, 218–19
  homeland and origins, 126, 218
  insurrection, 219
  neck bracelets, 136
  refugees, 11
Pagan, 190–91, 196, 202, 231
Palaung
  absorption of, 10
  agriculture and trade, 209, 224
  dress and jewellery, **73–4, 208,
    209**
  'Gold' and 'Silver', 72
  headmen, 210
  homeland and origins, 72, 196,
    209
  insurrection, 209
  population numbers, 199
  religion, 210
  society, 209
  villages and long-houses, **75**,
    209–10
Panthay (Hui-Hui)
  bound feet of women, **63**
  homeland and origins, 62, 208
Pegu, 154, 223
Phu Chaik (Grandfather-Buddha),
  222
Pin Ne Bang village, 72
Pindaya caves, Shan State, 182,
  183–4
Pwo, 120, 126, 221, 222
  see also Karen
Pyu, 196, 231

Rakhine
  absorbing neighbours, 11
  dress, **165**
  homeland and origins, 160, 196,
    223
  Muslim influence, 225–6
refugees, 11, 199, 222, 224
religion
  ancestor worship, 207, 209
  Buddhism, 76, 120, 210;
    hairs of the Buddha, 187;
    introduction of, 154, 160, 222,
    223; Kyaiktiyo pagoda, 154,
    155–7; Mahamuni Buddha image,
    11, 225; Mon, 224; Pindaya
    images, 184–5; reclining Buddha,
    190; Shwedagon Pagoda, 187,
    190, 232–3; Sule Pagoda, 187,
    188–9; Theravadha Buddhism,
    187, 206, 210, 224; wooden
    monasteries, 210
  Christian converts, 32, 120, 150,
    201, 207, 214, 221, 227
  fertility rites, 114
  Guisha cult, 107, 214
  man-god prophets, 107
  missionaries, 150, 214
  Muslims, 160
  Nat festival and shrines, 187,
    190, 191, 210, 221
  priest-exorcists (*mo kung*), 207
  shamans, 207, 214, 224
  spirit worship, 74, 120, 201,
    208, 209, 211; animism, 32,
    219, 221, 227; and Buddhism,
    187; Palaung spirit festival,
    210; spirit doctors, 209;
    spirit gates, 211–12; spirit
    headmen, 11; spirit houses,
    232; spirit masters, 144
  supernatural, 124, 206, 224
  Taoism, 208, 209
  Telakhon sect, 222
Riang
  dress and jewellery, **88–91**, 211,
    215
  homeland and origins, 87, 211
Rohingyas, 160

Salween River, 120
Saw Maung, General, 8
sawbwas (hereditary princes), 34,
  202, 204, 215, 216
Scott, Sir (James) George, 7, 80,
  101, 114, 211
Sgaw, 120, 126, 221, 222
  see also Karen
Shakama, *see* Thet
Shan State, 11, 196, 202–15
  Chinese immigration, 198
  ethnic groups, 196, 202
  Hsa-Htung sub-state, 210
  Kokang sub-state, 208
  Kuomintang invasion, 204
  liberated zones, 204
  nationalist insurrection, 202–5
  Taungyo people, 10
  see also Akha: Hmong: Intha:
    Lahu: Lisu: Palaung: Panthay:
    Pa-O: Riang: Shan (Tai): Yao
Shan (Tai), **35–7**
  absorbing neighbours, 10
  culture and language, 205
  ethnography, 205
  homeland and origins, 34, 196,
    205
  marriage ceremonies, 206
  migration to Thailand, 34, 205
  population numbers, 199

religion, 206
sawbwas (princes) administration,
  34, 196, 202, 204, 205
  social changes, 205
  tattooing, 206
Shin Byu (initiation rite), **186–7**
Shwedagon Pagoda, Rangoon, 187,
  190, 232–3
Singkaling Hkamti, 172, 177
Sittang River, 120
slavery, 202
Sule Pagoda, Rangoon, 187, **188–9**
Sumprabum River, 201

tattooing, 11, **124, 162, 166,
  169–71**, 206
Taunggyi, 198
Taungthu, *see* Pa-O
Taungyo
  dress and jewellery, **81–6**
  homeland and origins, 80, 210–11
  language, 211
  loss of tradition, 10
  Thailand, 10, 11, 198, 205, 206,
    207, 214, 219, 231, 232
thanaka paste, **36, 181**
Thaton, 76, 154, 223, 231
Thet, 11, 160, **161**, 225
Ton Pak village, 80
Toungoo, 196
travel
  mud roads, 8
  rivers, 199
  white, brown and black areas, 9

Vesali, 225
Vietnam, 206, 207

Wa
  absorption of, 10
  agriculture, 224
  dress and jewellery, **116–19, 217**
  head-hunters, 172, 216
  homeland and origins, 114, 196,
    215
  insurrection, 204, 216
  language, 215
  opium crop, 11, 215
  population numbers, 199, 215
  Wild Wa, **217**
Wunpawng, 200

Yang Sek, 211
Yang Wankum, 211
Yangtze River, 207
Yao
  agriculture, 206
  diaspora, 206
  dress and jewellery, **38–41**
  homeland and origins, 38, 206,
    207
  language, 206
  religion, 207
Yawyin, *see* Lisu, 208
Yellow River, 207
Yinbaw
  dress and jewellery, **151–3, 220**
  homeland and origins, 150, 220
  Kathowbow festival, 150
Yinnet, 10, 87, 211, *see also*
  Riang
Yinset, 10, 87, *see also* Riang
Young, William H. and Harold, 214

Zayein, *see* Lahta
Zomi, *see* Chin

First published in the United States in 1997 by
Amphoto Art, an imprint of Watson-Guptill Publications,
1515 Broadway, New York, NY 10036

First published in Great Britain in 1997
by Weidenfeld & Nicolson, a division of
The Orion Publishing Group Ltd
5 Upper Saint Martin's Lane
London WC2H 9EA

ISBN: 0-8174-5559-0

Edited by: Gillian Cribbs
The map on page 13 rendered by: Advanced Illustration
Designed by: Price Watkins
Printed in Italy
Set in: Sabon and Industrial 736 BT